Windows 10 Revealed

The Universal Windows Operating System for PC, Tablets, and Windows Phone

Kinnary Jangla

Apress®

Windows 10 Revealed

Kinnary Jangla
Bing Maps
San Francisco, California, USA

ISBN-13 (pbk): 978-1-4842-0687-4   ISBN-13 (electronic): 978-1-4842-0686-7
DOI 10.1007/978-1-4842-0686-7

Library of Congress Control Number: 2015948311

Managing Director: Welmoed Spahr
Lead Editor: Steve Anglin
Technical Reviewer: Kathleen Anderson
Editorial Board: Steve Anglin, Louise Corrigan, Jonathan Gennick, Robert Hutchinson,
    Michelle Lowman, James Markham, Susan McDermott, Matthew Moodie, Jeffrey Pepper,
    Douglas Pundick, Ben Renow-Clarke, Gwenan Spearing, Steve Weiss
Coordinating Editor: Mark Powers
Copy Editor: Kimberly Burton-Weisman
Compositor: SPi Global
Indexer: SPi Global
Artist: SPi Global

Distributed to the book trade worldwide by Springer Science+Business Media New York, 233 Spring Street, 6th Floor, New York, NY 10013. Phone 1-800-SPRINGER, fax (201) 348-4505, e-mail orders-ny@springer-sbm.com, or visit www.springeronline.com. Apress Media, LLC is a California LLC and the sole member (owner) is Springer Science + Business Media Finance Inc (SSBM Finance Inc). SSBM Finance Inc is a Delaware corporation.

For information on translations, please e-mail rights@apress.com, or visit www.apress.com.

Apress and friends of ED books may be purchased in bulk for academic, corporate, or promotional use. eBook versions and licenses are also available for most titles. For more information, reference our Special Bulk Sales–eBook Licensing web page at www.apress.com/bulk-sales.

Any source code or other supplementary material referenced by the author in this text is available to readers at www.apress.com/9781484206874. For detailed information about how to locate your book's source code, go to www.apress.com/source-code/.

Printed on acid-free paper

To my parents, Meena and Mukesh Jangla, for their everlasting love and support, and to my husband, Abhinav, for being the rock in my life.

Contents at a Glance

Contents

About the Author

Kinnary Jangla is an engineer and author with over seven years of experience in the technology industry and over ten years of experience in writing. Her first fiction-based novel, *Invisible Attires of the Mind (AuthorHouse, 2009)*, was published in 2008. She has worked for Toshiba Research, Internet Explorer, and Bing Search. Presently, she is employed as a software engineer with Bing Maps in Silicon Valley.

Kinnary has a master's degree in computer science from the University of Illinois at Chicago. Outside the world of technology and writing, Kinnary enjoys singing, painting, and outdoor activities.

About the Technical Reviewer

Kathleen Anderson was first honored with the Microsoft MVP award in October 2001. She has worked with FrontPage since 1997, Expression Web since Version 1, and has worked in the IT field for over 30 years. Kathleen recently retired from the State of Connecticut after 25 years of service, and has relocated to the beach in Oak Island, North Carolina. She served as the Core-CT Webmaster (www.core-ct.state.ct.us), and chaired the State of Connecticut's Committee on Web Site Accessibility. She owns a web design company, Spider Web Woman Designs (http://www.spiderwebwoman.com).

She was a technical editor on *Microsoft Expression Web 4 In Depth (Que Publishing, 2011), Sams Teach Yourself Microsoft Expression Web 4, Second Edition (Sams, 2012), Microsoft Expression Blend 4 Step by Step (Microsoft Press, 2011),* and *My Kindle Fire (Que Publishing, 2011).* She is known in some circles as the "FrontPage Database Wizard Queen" and in others as the "Accessibility Diva."

Acknowledgments

At Apress, I would like to thank Steve Anglin, editorial director, for giving me my first technical book, and Mark Powers, project manager, for being tremendously patient with my list of unending questions and the daily e-mails that spammed his inbox.

I would also like to thank the development editor, Matthew Moodie, and the technical reviewer, Kathleen Anderson, for reviewing this book so closely. Their feedback is what makes this book readable. I would also like to thank all the people involved in the making of this book that I didn't get a chance to work with, who are the actual makers of this book.

Lastly, I want to thank my family for their patience and belief in me. Their encouragement is what kept me going every day.

Introduction

What is Windows 10? What does Windows 10 look like on different devices? How can you upgrade to Windows 10? What can you expect from this book?

Windows 10 is the next generation of Windows and an evolution of the Windows 8 operating system, with a focus on transitioning between behaviors suitable for the type of device and the available input methods. The goal of Windows 10 is to unify Windows PC, Windows Phone, Surface, and Xbox One product families, along with upcoming new products, such as HoloLens. Windows 10 offers a fresh user interface on the tablet and PC, which is certainly a welcome change from the previous version of Windows where apps consumed the entire display and the Start menu took over the screen altogether. No more! Windows 10 brings back the familiarity. What's old is now new!

Windows 10 improves the user experience by adding a new revision of the Start menu on the desktop and tablet, and allows apps to run within the classic desktop mode and in full-screen mode. Windows 10 offers the concept of new universal apps. Some of these universal apps are bundled with Windows 10; they offer an innovative experience consistent across the device continuum for Office apps, Photos, Videos, Music, People, Mail, and Calendar. These apps have a new look and design, and feel the same from app to app and device to device. Content is stored and synced through OneDrive, enabling you to start somethings on one device and continue it on another, which makes it my personal favorite feature.

Windows 10 also integrates Cortana, the intelligent digital personal assistant—a notification system that can be synchronized between devices, and Edge, a new bundled web browser.

And above all, Windows 10 is a free upgrade from Windows 7, Windows 8, and Windows 8.1! Woot!

Note   The Microsoft term for apps is *Windows Store applications.* I'll just use *Windows apps* or often just *apps* throughout this book.

About this Book

This book is for the new and experienced Windows users who want to get a head start on navigating through the new user interface of the Windows 10 operating system on the phone, tablet, and PC. In this book, I explain how to upgrade to Windows 10 and emphasize what's new with the Windows 10 user interface on the phone, the tablet, and the PC. I also walk you through the all new integrated features—such as Cortana and Edge—that are common across all devices. There is a dedicated chapter on universal apps, which will help you use and sync your apps on all of your Windows 10 devices.

What Do You Need to Know Before You Read this Book?

You need to have a Windows 10–compatible device with either Windows 10 already installed or a previous version of Windows that can be upgraded to Windows 10. If you have used Windows 7 or Windows 8 before, Windows 10 will be very familiar to you since it is a good mix of the classic desktop of Windows 7 and the metro apps mode of Windows 8. If you are a first-time user of Windows, then you simply need to want to learn Windows 10!

Note Microsoft uses the term *user interface*, which means everything that is visual on the Windows operating system. I simply use *UI* throughout this book for simplicity.

How Is this Book Structured?

I have divided this book into four chapters, as I summarize next. The four topics make for the building blocks of Windows 10. I go deeply into each of these five topics and summarize at the end of each chapter what you should be comfortable trying. There are also some important notes and tips that I emphasize for you to read and make note.

The first chapter tells you what is to come in the following chapters, how the book is structured, and what you need to know before reading. The second chapter is focused on Windows 10 phones and small devices. This chapter talks about the changes in the mobile UI and some of the new features that stand out in small devices. The third chapter is all about Windows 10 tablets and PCs. Here you will learn everything you need to start being productive on your Windows 10 surface and desktop. The fourth chapter is common to all devices. They are based on some of the features that have never been on the Windows operating system.

I focus on the basic user interface differences between Windows 10 and previous versions of Windows. I am not going to talk about features in the OS that already existed in previous versions. For example, I will assume that you already know what a metro app in Windows 8 is and what the Windows 7 classic desktop looks like.

I have deliberately separated the chapters on phones, small devices, tablets, and PCs to keep things clear and simple. I have taken a relaxed approach by throwing in pictures wherever a UI is explained, because I truly believe pictures speak louder than words. This is a primer to get you started on this new version of Windows and show you how to make the best use of new built-in features, such as Cortana and universal apps, efficiently. There are a lot of different topics that were impossible to fit into such a mini version of this book. Hence, I have tried to focus on immediate user productivity and have detailed only the major building blocks of Windows 10.

The following sections summarize the chapters in this book.

Getting Started

I give you a brief overview of the revamped features of Windows 10 and the new features it has bundled with it for the very first time. After reading this chapter, you will understand what to expect in the upcoming chapters and get a brief overview of what is different in Windows 10 from the previous versions of Windows.

Chapter 1: Windows 10 for Phones and Small Devices

In this chapter, I talk about the Windows 10 UI, mainly for Windows Phone and small tablets. Whereas it's still called Windows 10 on phones, it's really a version that's optimized for smaller screens. I break this chapter into three main sections—namely the Start screen, the Action Center, and the most refreshing interactive notifications. This chapter explains all that is new in these areas in terms of UI and functionality. By the end of this chapter, you should be able to play around with the revamped Start screen on your phone, be familiarized with the increased number of quick actions available in the Action Center, and be able to respond to your messages and e-mails straight from the Start screen.

Chapter 2: Windows 10 for Tablets and Desktops

Windows 10 has a very fresh feel on tablets and PCs. In this chapter, I show you—with the help of screenshots—the integration of the classic desktop and the metro-style apps. I show you how Windows 10 beautifully recognizes its continuum feature between the tablet and the PC modes. I go a little deeper into the revamped Start menu and explain where the missing charms bar went. This chapter will give you a great handle on navigating through the new Windows 10 UI on tablets. By the end of this chapter, you should have a great sense of the new Windows 10 UI on your desktop or surface, and be able to navigate through the Start menu seamlessly, play around with virtual desktops, and get going with your device.

Chapter 3: Cortana and Edge

Cortana and Edge run across all devices in a similar fashion. So this chapter is common to phones, tablets, and PCs. Cortana, the intelligent digital personal assistant, is there to help make things easier for you and keep you up-to-date on the things that matter to you the most. In this chapter, you will learn more things that you can do efficiently with the help of Cortana, and understand how to best customize it to meet your needs. Edge—the new Windows 10 built-in browser—is available on the phone, the tablet, and the PC. It has a completely new engine, different from Internet Explorer, and gives you a richer reading experience along with the ability to customize the page you're viewing. By the end of this chapter you should be able to use Cortana with speech and text, and to browse through web pages and customize them to meet your needs.

Chapter 4: Universal Apps

Having one experience across all your devices is a big part of Windows 10. In this chapter I tell you more about the free built-in Office apps that sync across your phone, tablet, and PC. I show you how the rich functionality of Microsoft Word, Excel, and PowerPoint are available on all of your devices. Along with these apps, I talk about some other bundled apps—like Mail, Calendar, Photos, and Maps—and show you how they make your life more convenient. By the end of this chapter you should be able to play around with all the built-in universal apps on all of your devices, and have a sense of everything you can achieve by efficiently using them—making your life a lot easier.

CHAPTER 1

Windows 10 for Phones and Small Devices

In this chapter, I show you how to use some of the features that you are more likely to use on your Windows Phone 10. However, all of these features can be used on all qualifying Windows 10 devices. Other features that are common to all devices are covered in later chapters. Here I will show you how to navigate through and interact with your new Windows Phone 10. I define and elaborate on the features that form the core of the Windows 10 operating system on the phone and small devices.

You may already be familiar with the Windows 8 user interface for phones. Windows 10 is very similar to Windows 8. That means lots and lots of tiles, but more refreshing. I do not go into the details of the Windows Phone 8 user interface in this book. There is a lot of good information about Windows Phone 8 and its features available in Wikipedia and MSDN, which have balanced and insightful descriptions.

If you don't already know much about Windows 8, or you haven't used a Windows phone before, I highly recommend reading up on the previous versions of Windows to see how the operating system has evolved in the past few years. I am a screenshot zealot, and I believe that visual images are way simpler to understand than having to interpret explanations. To that end, you will find a lot of pictures interspersed with explanations everywhere in this chapter and all that follow.

In this chapter I focus on defining and explaining a feature, and follow it with simple steps, each associated with a screenshot to guide you through using that feature on your own phone. I start slowly, by showing you the new ways you can customize your Start screen, and then I build up on that to demonstrate different features. I then show you how you can use the new expanded view in the Action Center and use the quick links for efficiency. I also show you how to interact with the new notifications on your screen without having to go to the apps themselves. Table 1-1 provides a summary of this chapter.

© Kinnary Jangla 2015
K. Jangla, *Windows 10 Revealed*, DOI 10.1007/978-1-4842-0686-7_1

Table 1-1. *Chapter Summary*

Problem	Figure
Apply a background image to the Start screen	1-1 to 1-8
View your recently downloaded apps	1-9
Interact with the new Action Center	1-10
Interact with notifications	1-11 to 1-13
Other features of Windows Phone 10	1-14 to 1-21

▨ **Note** I am going to use the Nokia Lumia 830 phone on the AT&T network for the screenshots throughout this chapter. However, all of these features apply to all qualifying Windows Phone 10 devices.

Apply a Background Image to the Start Screen

At the heart of the new Windows operating system are tiles. On your new Windows Phone 10 you will notice that the tiles on the Start screen are transparent. If you love having images in the background, even while you are on your Start screen, you're set! You can set your favorite photo as the background on your Start screen. Scrolling over to the program list, you continue to see the transparency. If you don't like the transparency, you can always go back to a black background. Any image you choose for the background now extends to the corners of the screen in a full-bleed layout. You can also organize tiles, pin or unpin them, move them around, and change their sizes the same way you did in Windows 8.

Now I'll show you how you can set a photo from your Photos app as the background image of your Start screen.

1. On your Windows Phone 10, find the Settings app, as shown in Figure 1-1. (If you can't find it on the Start screen, scroll to the right and find it in the program list, as shown in Figure 1-2).

Figure 1-1. *The Settings app on the Start screen*

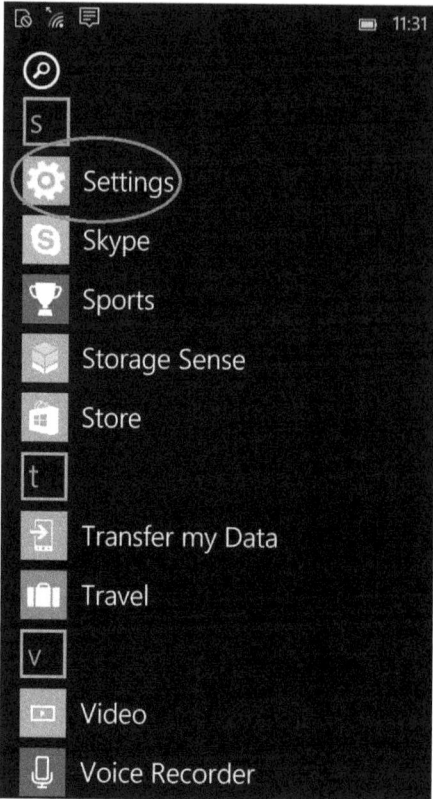

Figure 1-2. *The Settings app in the program list*

2. In the Settings app, select **Personalization** (see Figure 1-3) followed by **Background** (see Figure 1-4).

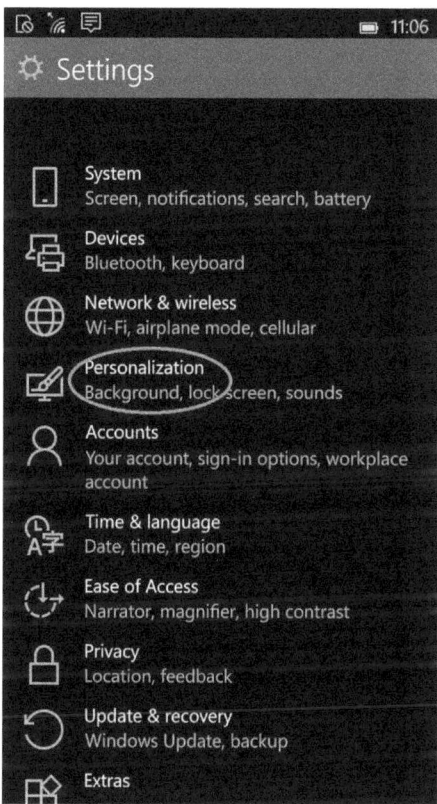

Figure 1-3. *Selecting Personalization in Settings*

Figure 1-4. *Selecting Background within Personalization*

3. After you tap **Background**, select **Browse** (see Figure 1-5), which takes you to your Photos app. Select a photo from your collection and then select the tick mark on the bottom of the screen (see Figure 1-6).

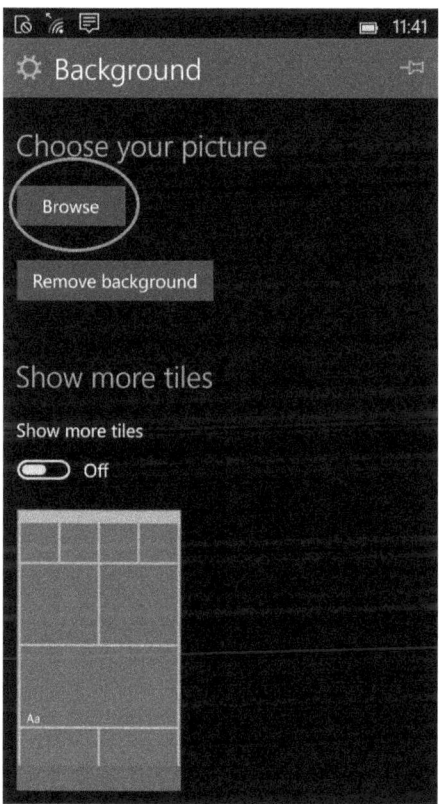

Figure 1-5. *Tapping Browse within Background*

Figure 1-6. *Selecting a photo*

4. This takes you back to the Background screen and you can
    see your image set as the background, as seen in Figure 1-7.
    If you go to your Start screen afterward, you'll see that the tiles
    are transparent, and you can now see your favorite image in
    the background (see Figure 1-8).

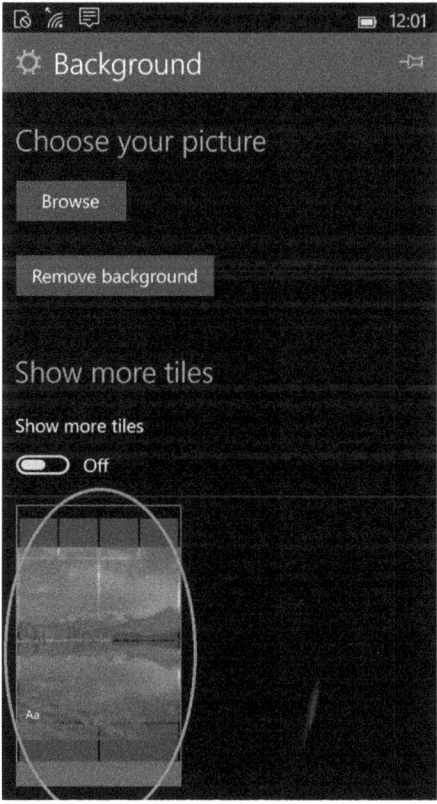

Figure 1-7. *Indicates that image has been set as the background*

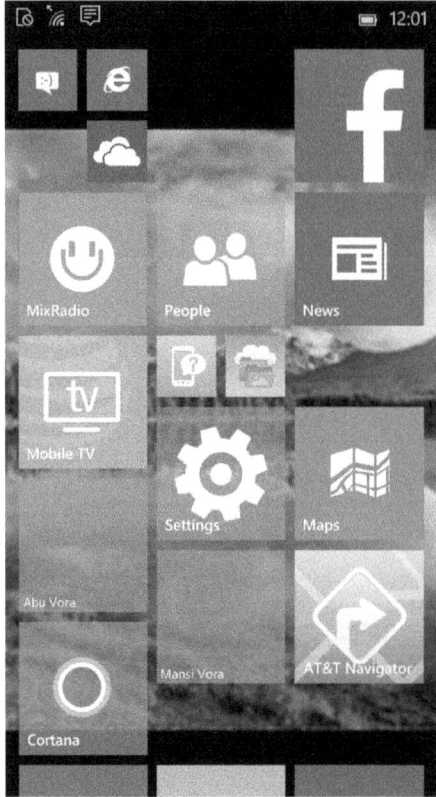

Figure 1-8. *Image has been set as the background on the Start screen*

View Your Recently Downloaded Apps

Any apps that you download can be seen in the recently downloaded apps section on top of the program list. Figure 1-9 gives you a preview of the recently downloaded apps section.

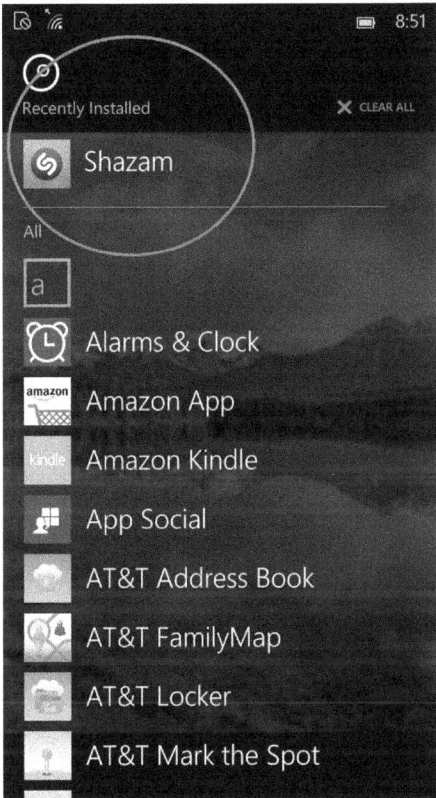

Figure 1-9. *The Shazam app is recently downloaded and can be seen on the top section of the program list*

Interact with the New Action Center

The Action Center in Windows is a central place to view alerts and notifications. It lists all the maintenance messages that help you take actions so that Windows continues to run smoothly. The new Action Center in Windows 10 has many more quick links than Windows 8 had. Tapping to expand in the Action Center should show you all the available actions that you can quickly perform (see Figure 1-10). These quick links are extremely useful and let you do the job straight from the Action Center. Using the quick links, you can set Do-Not-Disturb hours, set your VPN, use your camera, change your screen's brightness, open your Wi-Fi and Bluetooth settings, and share your internet.

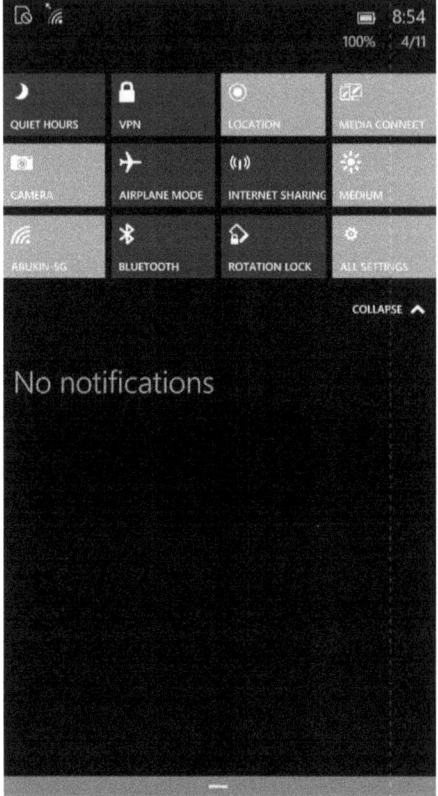

Figure 1-10. *Tap to expand and see all the quick links*

To open the Action Center, swipe from top to bottom anywhere on your phone.

Interactive Notifications in the New Action Center

One of the useful tricks in Windows 10 is the ability to expand notifications in the Action Center. You can see a little down arrow on each of your notifications; this can be tapped. When you initiate the arrow, the full snippet expands, revealing the entire notification, as seen in Figure 1-11. Even better, the OS dims the other notifications, bringing the current one to the forefront.

Figure 1-11. *Tapping a notification shows you the full subject text*

With message notifications, you can directly reply to the message from the Action Center, as seen in Figure 1-12.

Figure 1-12. *Reply directly to a text message by tapping the notification*

Notifications can also be easily deleted and removed from the Action Center by swiping right to left, as seen in Figure 1-13.

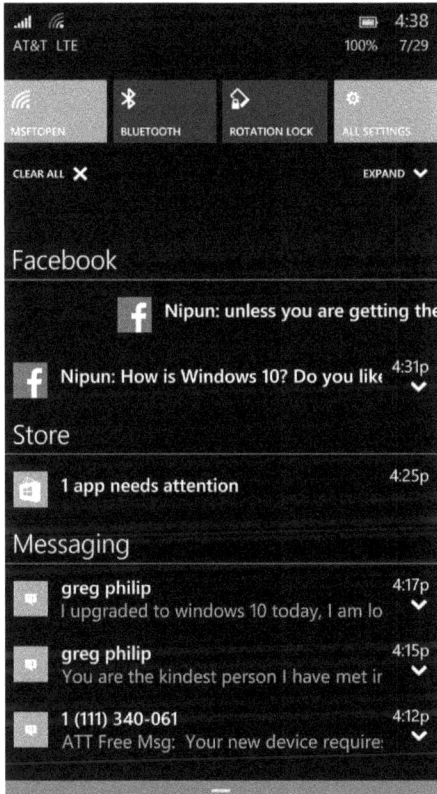

Figure 1-13. *Delete notifications by swiping right to left*

Some Other Features

Here I list some other interesting and improved features of Windows 10. The following features either have a refined user interface or some cool, newly added features that I thought were worth mentioning.

Phone Dialer

One of the features that is unique to the phone is the dialer. The phone dialer has tremendously improved from the previous versions of Windows Phone. Now the dialer searches for your contacts while you're dialing the number. Start punching in a number (see Figure 1-14), better yet, a name (see Figure 1-15), and the dialer automatically searches your phone book and shows you the contacts that match the fragment you've typed in. This greatly enhances your telephonic experience since you are now confident that the dialer will surely be able to find your contact.

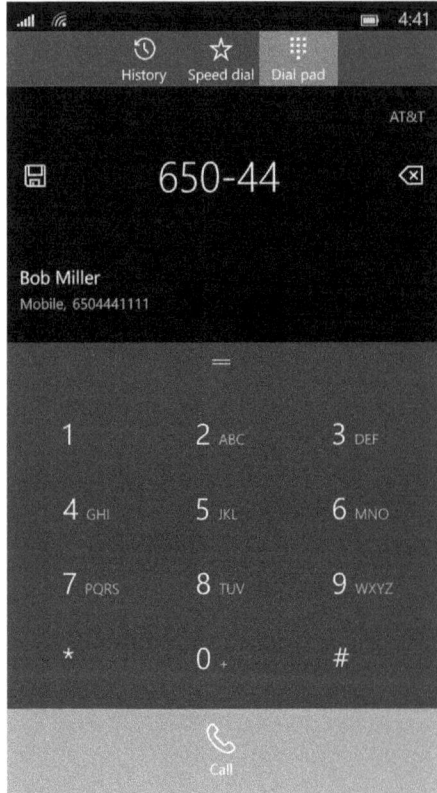

Figure 1-14. The new enhanced dialer. It searches for your contact as you punch in the number

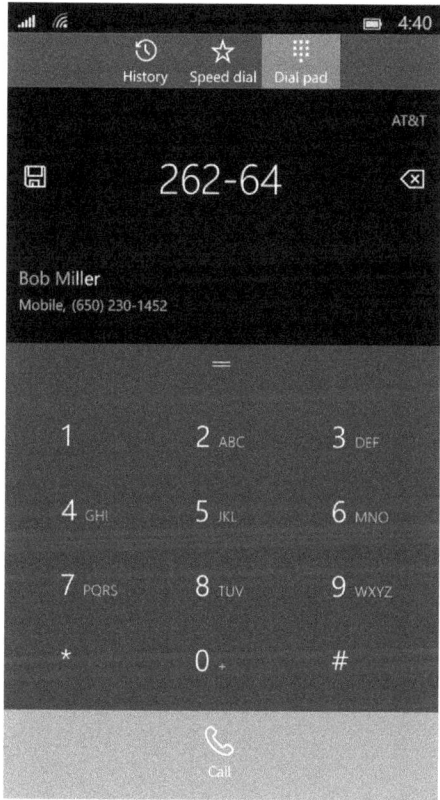

Figure 1-15. *The new enhanced dialer. It searches for your contact as you punch in the name of the contact*

Visual Voicemail

Visual voicemail implementation makes things easier. While it is a very basic feature, it was much needed in the Windows Phones—and it's here now! You can now see the name or number of the person who left you a voicemail, hear the message, call the person back, and/or delete the message from the voicemail screen (see Figure 1-16).

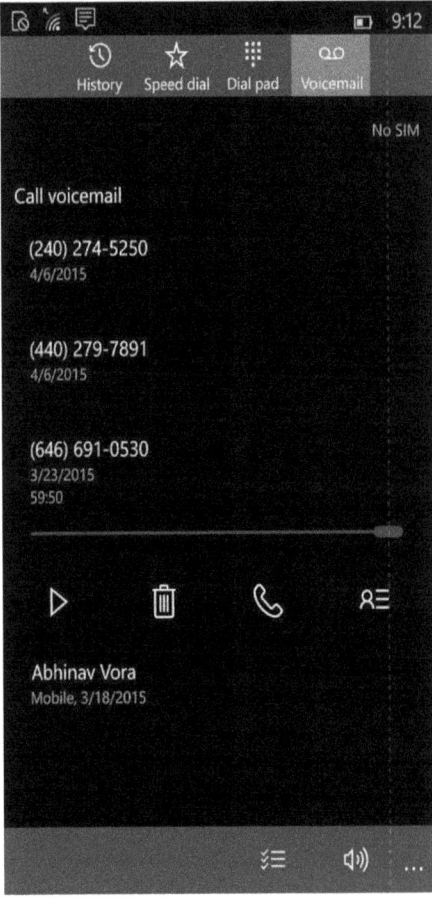

Figure 1-16. *Visual Voicemail screen*

Messaging

The next app that logically comes to mind is the Messaging app. This app integrates Skype chat and makes chatting more fun. There are also some stylistic changes in the app, which greatly enhances your experience. It also makes calling someone a lot easier. Directly from the messaging window, you see a phone icon that allows you to make a call (see Figure 1-17). When I'm super busy, I usually prefer calling someone. The Messaging app makes it very quick to do.

Figure 1-17. *Call directly from the Messaging app*

Maps

Windows Phone 10 comes with a beautiful maps experience. My favorite feature here allows you to download maps offline. During my free time, I love going for hikes in remote places, but there is usually no network available on my phone. The offline maps work beautifully at such places. To download an offline map, you can simply go to Settings ➤ System ➤ Maps. On your Maps menu, you'll see **Map updates** and an option to download offline maps. Once you select your region, the map starts downloading onto your phone. This means that when you are in remote locations, you don't need the Internet, GPS, or your phone to connect to your data network. You can use the downloaded map on your phone. The following screenshots show you how to download an offline map from your Windows Phone 10 Settings app.

Let's consider an example. Last Sunday I went for a hike around Bodega Bay in California with a few friends. I am new to the state and not great with directions, so I decided to download the entire California map in case I experienced loss of network, either while driving or while hiking. This is how I did it.

1. I went to the Maps app and selected **Download a map** (see Figure 1-18).

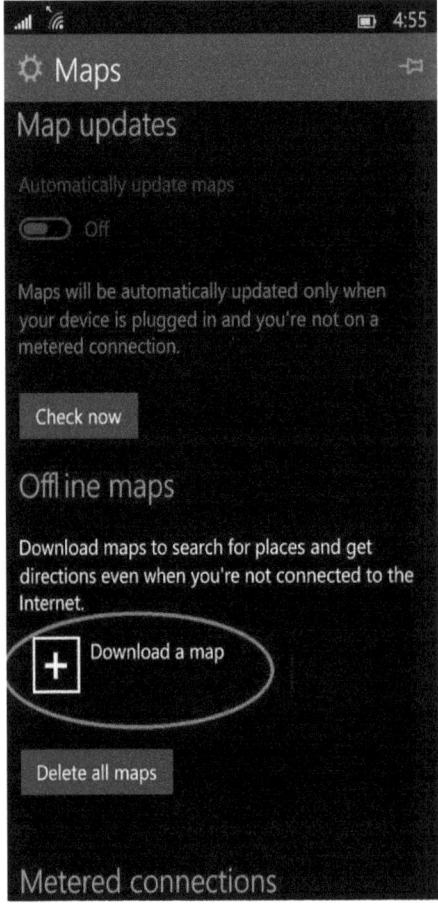

Figure 1-18. *Tap "Download a map" to download a map of the region you are interested in*

2. That got me to the next screen, where I selected a region; here it was **USA** (see Figure 1-19).

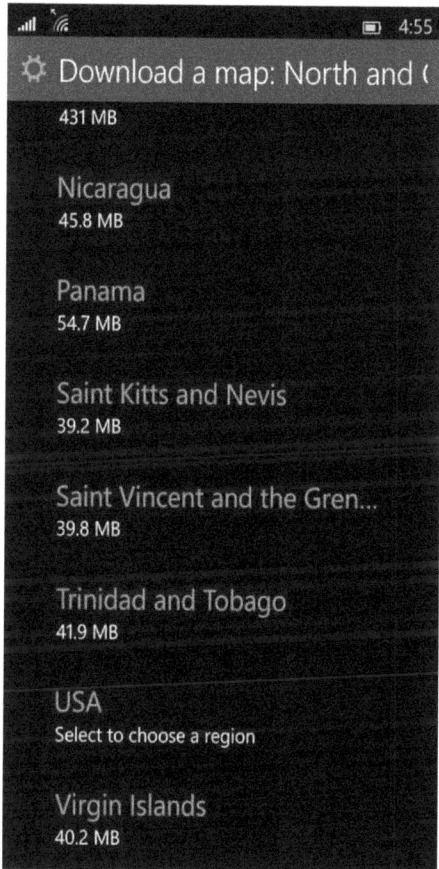

Figure 1-19. *Select a region*

3. After selecting a region, I chose a state; in this case it was **California** (see Figure 1-20).

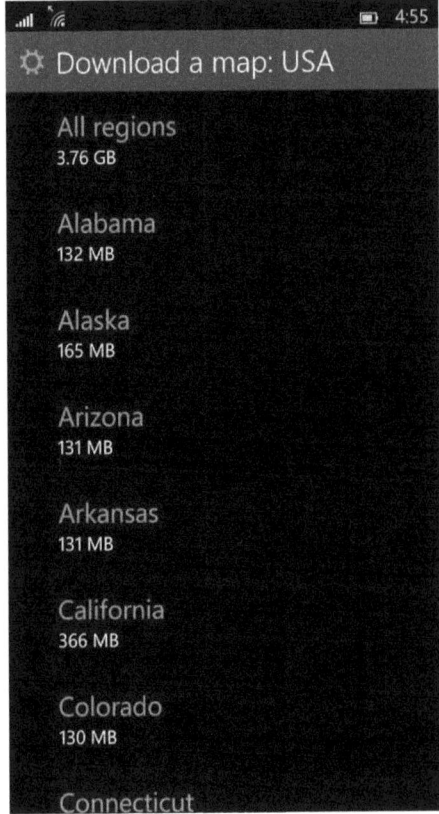

Figure 1-20. *Select the state*

4. That got me to the screen shown in Figure 1-21, displaying the
    progress bar of my California map download.

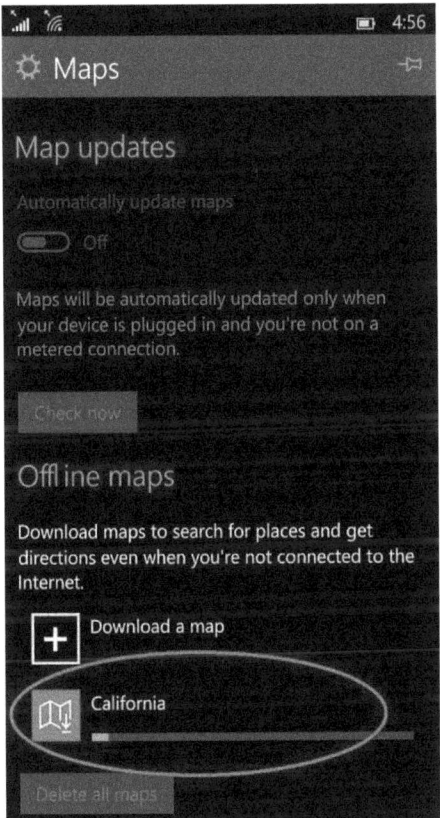

Figure 1-21. *The progress bar of the download*

Driving Mode

Windows Phone 10 also has an integrated driving mode. This means that you can block off your texts, calls, and any other notifications that usually bother you while driving. I am greatly against texting while driving and I dislike any distractions. I love this feature because enabling it on my Windows phone blocks off all my notifications. Go to Settings ➤ System ➤ Driving Mode. Once you're there, you will see the screen in Figure 1-22.

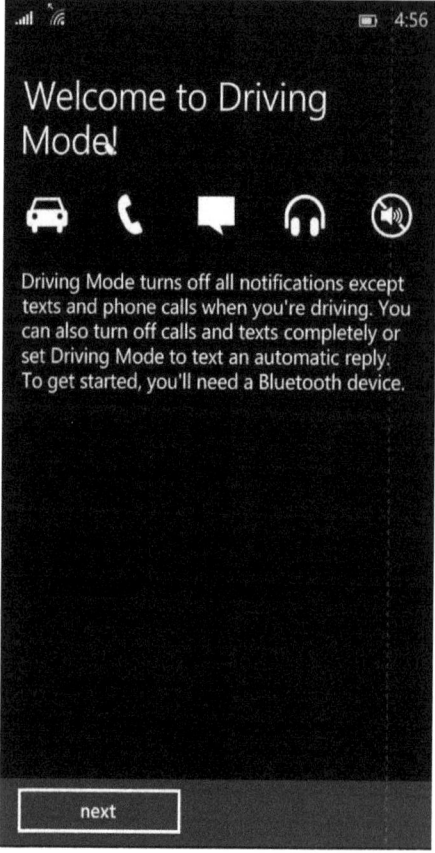

Figure 1-22. *Driving Mode enabled*

Press the **next** button on the screen to go to the setup screen (see Figure 1-23).

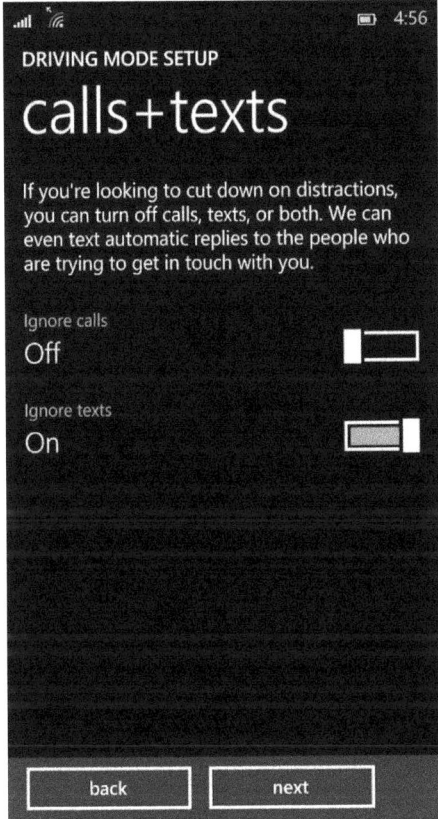

Figure 1-23. *Blocking off text and calls*

The People app is greatly restyled and its experience is similar across all devices. In Chapter 4 I go into the depths of the People, Calendar, Mail, and Photos apps.

Other Windows 10 features, such as Edge and Cortana, have dedicated chapters since they are brand-new features. They also have a similar experience across all devices.

☐ **Tip**　The preceding features can be used on tablets and desktops as well. I am explaining these particular features on the phone based on what you are more likely to use on the phone than on larger devices.

Wrapping It Up

In this chapter, I showed you how to set a background image on your Start screen so that you can view your favorite photo through the transparent tiles. I also showed you how to use the quick links in the Action Center to view your notification snippets and interact with them efficiently. I also showed you how to use some of the other features that are unique to the phone, such as the dialer and the revamped Messaging app. I walked you through how to download a map of your geographical region for offline access and how to switch to Driving Mode on your new Windows Phone 10. In the next chapter, I'll show you how to use some of the features that you are more likely to use on tablets and desktops.

■ **Note**   Windows 10 is all about unity. The operating system strives to give the user the same experience across devices. None of these features are unique to any one device. All apps and features look and feel similar on all of your Windows 10 devices. The key thing to know about Windows Phone 10 is that although the operating system is optimized for a smaller screen, it's still considered Windows 10.

CHAPTER 2

Windows 10 for Tablets and Desktops

In this chapter, I show you how to use some of the features of Windows 10 that you are more likely to use on a touch-based tablet or a desktop. However, as I have mentioned throughout the first chapter, all the features can be used on all qualifying Windows 10 devices. Here I will show you how to navigate through and interact with your new Windows 10 touch tablet and desktop. I will show you how, with the Windows 10 Continuum feature, your experience will differ depending upon whether you are using a tablet or a PC. I will also explain in depth about how the revamped Start menu actually works.

The Start menu in Windows 10 is very interesting. It's somewhere in between the classic menu from the older versions of Windows and the recent metro menu from Windows 8. It's a perfect middle ground for a user who wants to use the Windows 10 device both in the Tablet mode and the Desktop mode. Later in this chapter, I explain the different swipe gestures.

If you have ever used any version of Windows, this new operating system will bring some amount of familiarity. And if you've specifically used Windows 8, Windows 10 will be much more familiar to you. Windows 10 is a great mix of Windows 7 and Windows 8. The classic desktop user gets the Start menu back in its original position, and the Windows 8 tablet user gets the full Start screen. This version of Windows brings with it lots of good UI changes, refreshing looks, and tons of new features to increase your productivity.

As in the previous chapter, I explain a feature and provide easy-to-follow steps for you to learn it. I mix in screenshots every now and then to make sure that you interpret the explanation and the steps correctly. These visualizations make following the steps much easier. I slowly start with the newly introduced Continuum feature, and then go a little deeper to explain the Start menu. I end the chapter by showing you the swipe gestures that can be used on a tablet. Table 2-1 provides a summary of this chapter.

© Kinnary Jangla 2015
K. Jangla, *Windows 10 Revealed*, DOI 10.1007/978-1-4842-0686-7_2

Table 2-1. *Chapter Summary*

Problem	Figures
Continuum feature: Tablet and PC mode	2-1 to 2-5
Start menu: In depth	2-6 to 2-18
Swipe gestures	2-19

≡ **Note** Throughout this chapter I am going to use *Desktop mode* and *PC mode* interchangeably. They both share the same meaning.

Continuum Feature: Tablet and PC Modes

The new Continuum feature that debuts in Windows 10 helps the operating system work well with devices that support both a mouse and keyboard, and touch input, like Microsoft's Surface tablet. It provides an intelligent way for Windows 10 to understand the operating mode required by its user. For convertible devices there are two modes: Tablet and Desktop. When you want to use the device as a tablet, the Tablet mode changes the operating system so that it is more touch-friendly. Once you connect a mouse and keyboard, or flip your laptop around, it switches automatically to Desktop mode. Apps turn back into desktop windows that are easier to move around. In the world of touch, non-touch and hybrid, this operating system caters to multiple preferences. When you close an app in Tablet mode, you are taken back to the Start screen instead of the desktop.

Switching between modes is as easy as connecting or disconnecting your peripherals and choosing your mode from the pop-up alert. The Continuum feature gives you a great experience on your convertible devices and it works seamlessly.

Now I'll show you how your experience differs in a Tablet mode compared to a PC mode. I'll start by showing how to switch between the two modes. You can switch between the Tablet mode and the PC mode by selecting or deselecting the **Tablet mode** tab in the Notifications Center, which you can bring up by clicking on the little Notifications tray on the bottom right of your screen while in Desktop mode.

When in Desktop mode, you can switch to the Tablet mode using the following methods.

In this method, you can switch between modes by bringing up the Notifications Center and selecting the tray icon on the taskbar, as described in the following steps.

1. Select the tray in the right corner of the taskbar, as seen in Figure 2-1.

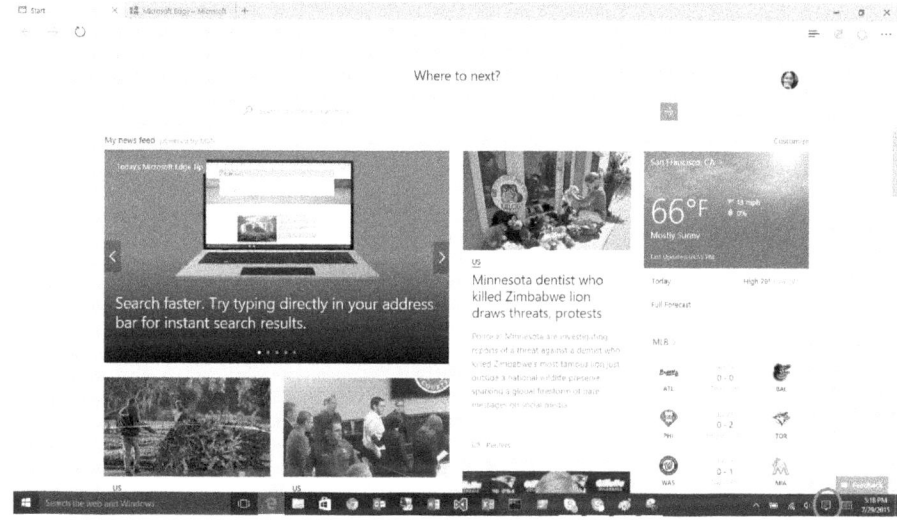

Figure 2-1. *Selecting the tray icon on the right corner of the taskbar to open the Notifications Center*

> 2. Select **Tablet mod**e from the Notifications Center, as seen in Figure 2-2.

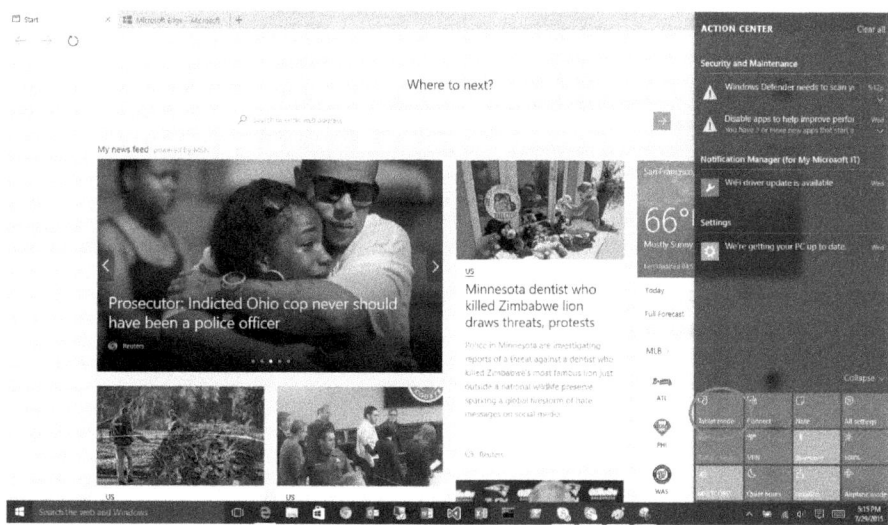

Figure 2-2. *Selecting Tablet mode from the Notifications Center*

■ **Note** To switch from Tablet mode to Desktop mode, you can use this method and unselect the Tablet mode from the Notifications Center. This will switch your device to Desktop mode.

Tablet Mode

Once you are in Tablet mode, your device is going to customize its behavior accordingly to enhance your experience in this mode. Some features behave differently in Tablet mode than they do in Desktop mode. The Start menu opens as a full screen when in Tablet mode. Similarly, all apps open in full screen when in Tablet mode. Figure 2-3 shows what the Start menu looks like in Tablet mode. Figure 2-4 shows what the apps look like when opened in Tablet mode.

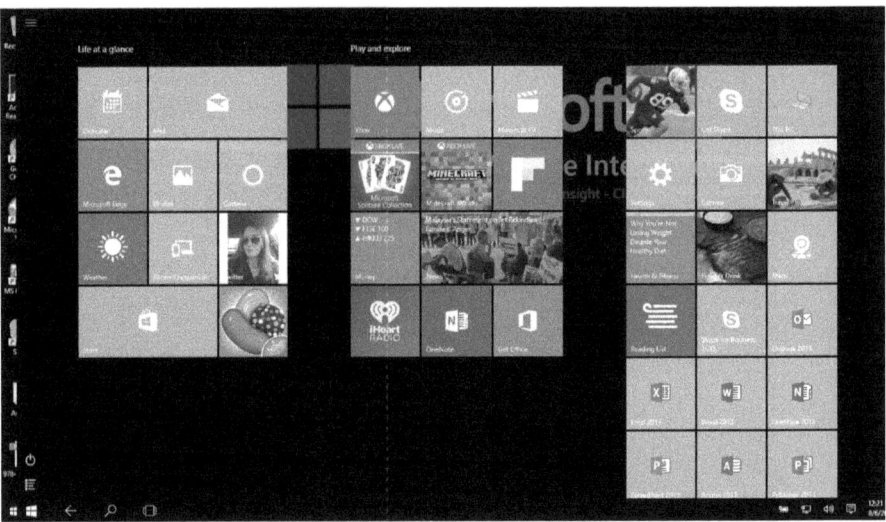

Figure 2-3. Open the Start menu in Tablet mode

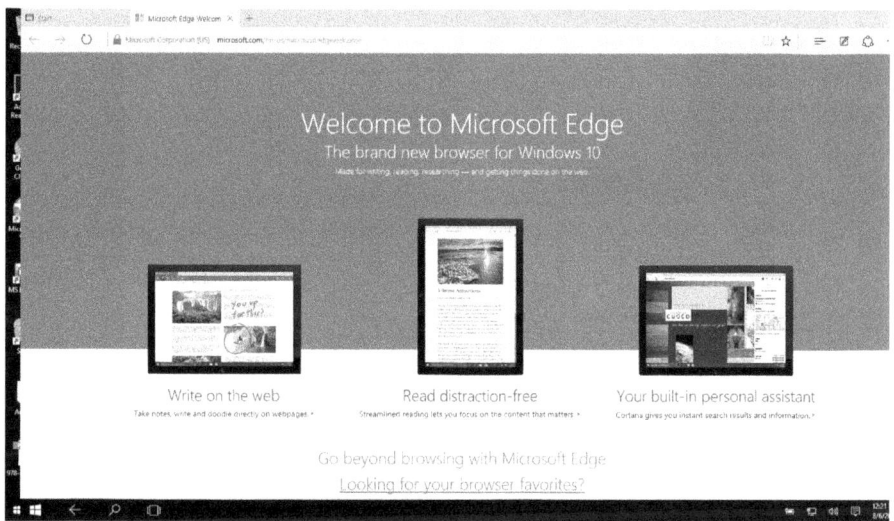

Figure 2-4. *Apps (here the Microsoft Edge browser app) opens in full-screen mode*

Desktop Mode

You can switch to Desktop mode by unselecting Tablet mode. Once in Desktop mode, your Start menu is no longer in full screen and you can view it in its original position, as in the classic versions of Windows. Your apps will no longer be in full screen either. They'll open in desktop windows as soon as you switch your mode. Figure 2-5 shows what the Start menu and the apps look like in Desktop mode.

31

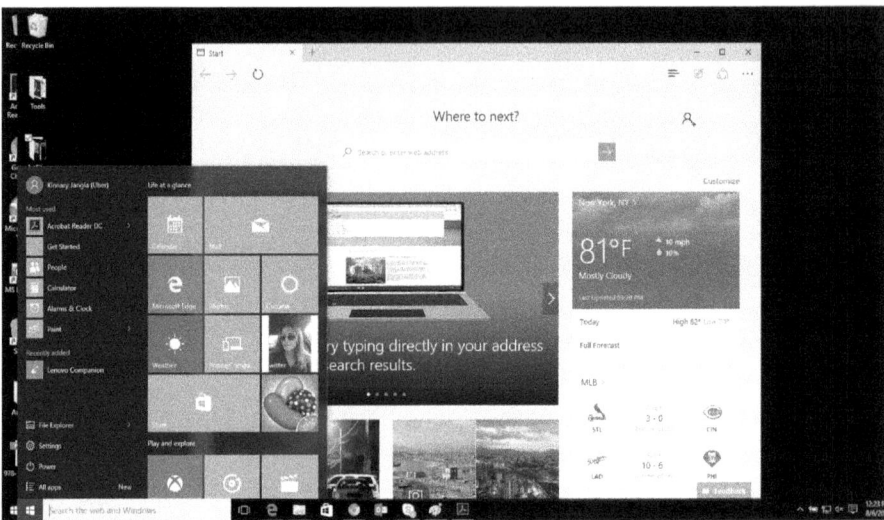

Figure 2-5.   The Start menu in Desktop mode is not full screen. Apps open in desktop windows

Start Menu: In Depth

The Windows 10 Start menu is revamped; it is a refreshing change from the classic Windows 7 Start menu. If you've used Windows 7 before, you'll see the return of the Start menu in its original position, except that it's much better. If you've been a Windows 8 user, the Windows 10 Start menu will be familiar. It's an efficient integration of the Windows 7 Start menu and the Windows 8 Start screen. The left side of the Start menu has a list of apps divided into different categories; the right side is the modern version of the Start screen, where you can pin your apps for quick access. As I have shown you, the Start menu resizes itself, depending upon whether the device is in Tablet mode or PC mode. There are lots of different customizations that you can do with the Start menu. I'm going to divide it into the following sections for clarity.

Pin and Unpin Tiles

"Pinning apps to Start" pins an app to the right side of the Start menu. That way you can access your apps very easily in both Tablet mode and Desktop mode. To pin an app to the Start menu as a tile, find the app in the Start menu, right-click it, and click **Pin to Start**. To unpin a tile from the Start menu, right-click the tile, and click **Unpin from Start**. I show you how to do both in the next section.

Pin to Start

Let's start by pinning to Start.

1. Navigate to your favorite app in the apps list (here I choose the Music app) and right-click, as seen in Figure 2-6.

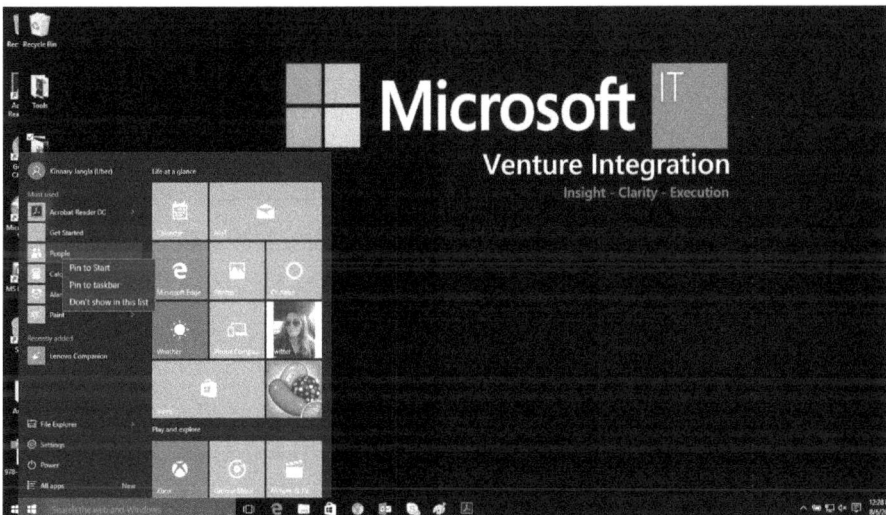

Figure 2-6. *Go to your favorite app and right-click on it*

2. Select the **Pin to Start** option, as seen in Figure 2-7. The app gets pinned to the right side of the Start menu.

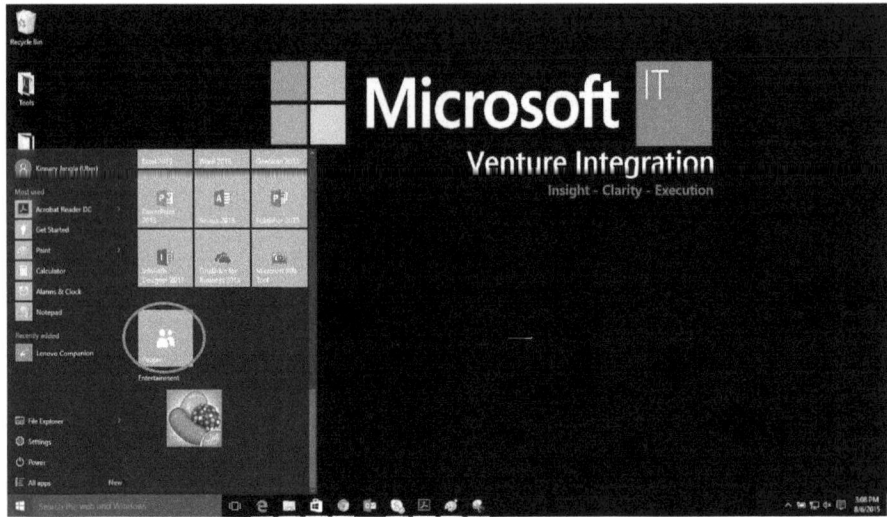

Figure 2-7. *Select the Pin to Start option. The People app is pinned to the right side of the Start menu*

Unpin from Start

Here I show you how to unpin an app from the Start menu.

1. To unpin the app from the Start menu, simply right-click on the pinned app.

2. You will see the context menu. Select the **Unpin from Start** option, as seen in Figure 2-8. The app will be unpinned from the Start menu.

Figure 2-8. *Unpin app from the Start menu*

Resize and Move Tiles

Like in Windows 8, Windows 10 lets you play around with your tiles. You can resize your tiles, move them around, and arrange them however you like. Depending upon the tile, you will be able to click it, hold it, and drag it around the Start menu. Now I will show you how to resize a tile.

1. To resize a tile, right-click it and hover over **Resize** until the resize menu shows up, as seen in Figure 2-9.

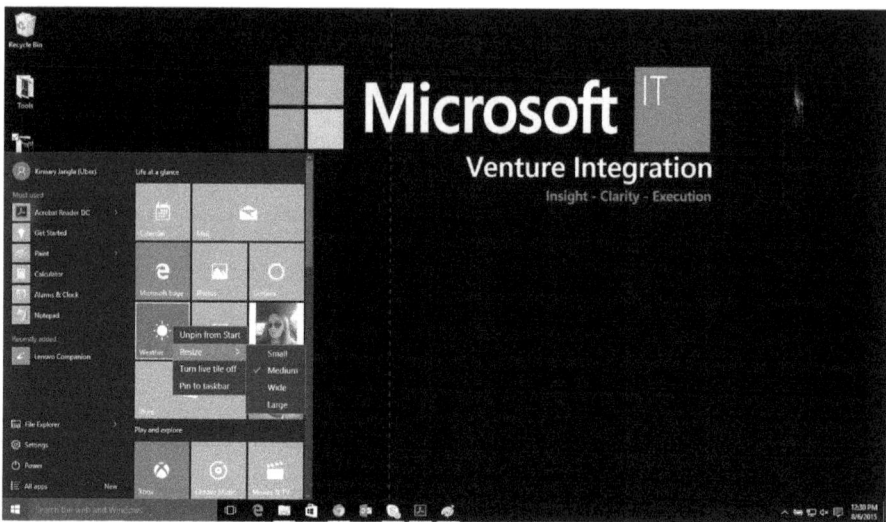

Figure 2-9. *Right-click the app and hover over the Resize menu*

2. Select one of the sizes—Small or Medium. The tile size changes, as seen in Figure 2-10.

Figure 2-10. *The app size tile changes to wide*

Edit the Tiles Section and Create New Categories

Like in Windows 8, in Windows 10, you can divide your live tiles into different categories. You can also edit the default categories and rename them whatever you want. I will now show you how to create a new category and how to edit an existing category.

Create a New Category

To create a new category, do the following:

1. Click a tile, hold it, and drag it to the bottom of the Start menu until a black bar shows up, as seen in Figure 2-11. Drop the tile below the black bar. Your tile will end up in its own little section.

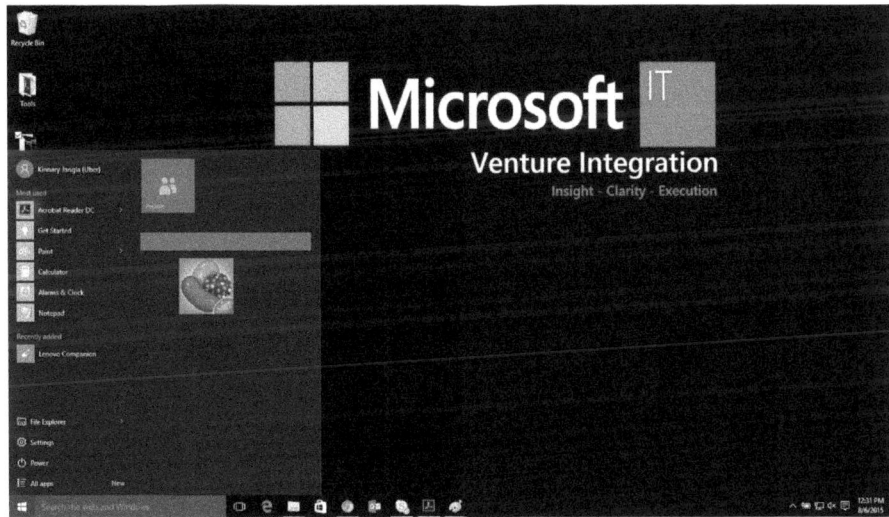

Figure 2-11. *Hold and drag an app to the bottom of the Start menu. Drop the app below the new dull black bar that appears*

2. Click the area above the tile (where you saw the black bar). A white outline will appear, as seen in Figure 2-12. Start typing in this box to name your category.

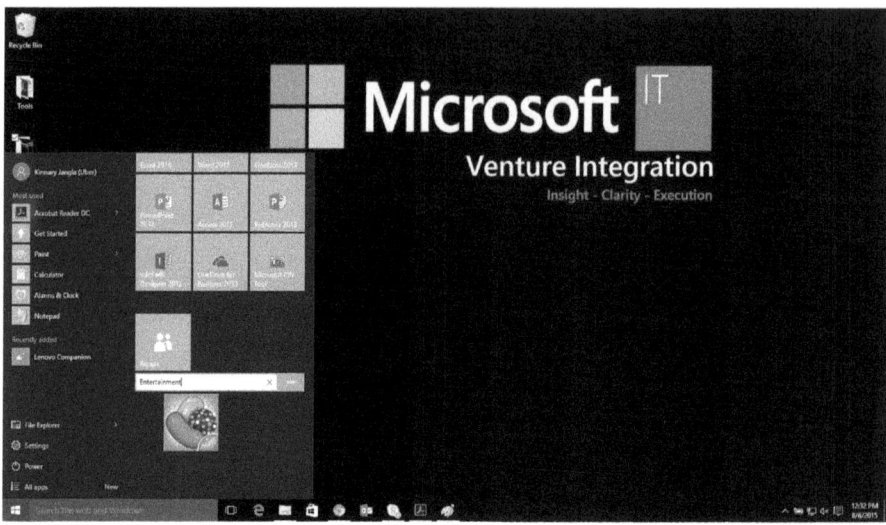

Figure 2-12. *Click the area above the app. A white line appears. Name the category.*
(I have named it Entertainment)

Edit an Existing Category

To rename a category, do the following:

1. Click a category name to highlight it, as seen in Figure 2-13.

Figure 2-13. *Click the Life at a glance category name until a white text box appears*

2. Start typing to edit it, as seen in Figure 2-14.

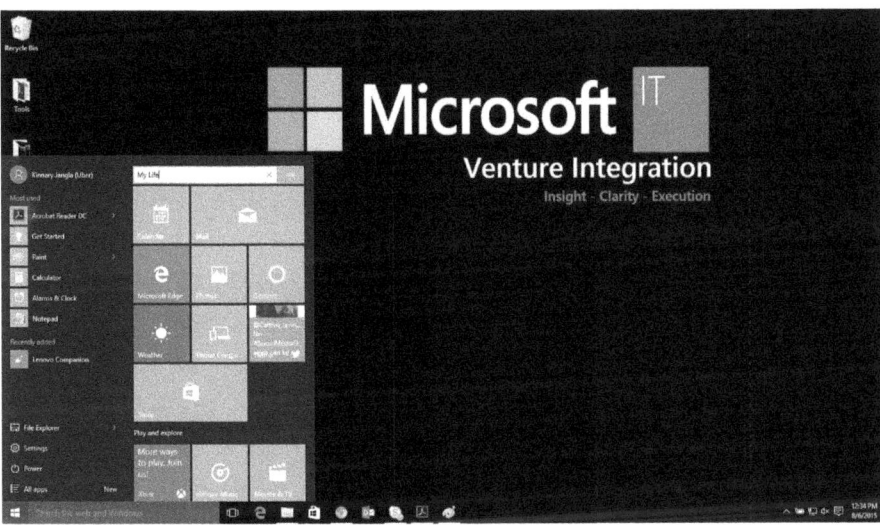

Figure 2-14. Renaming Life at a glance to My Life

Most Recently Used Apps

The most recently and frequently used apps are placed under the Most Used section on the left side of the Start menu (see Figure 2-15). This list has all the apps that you use frequently.

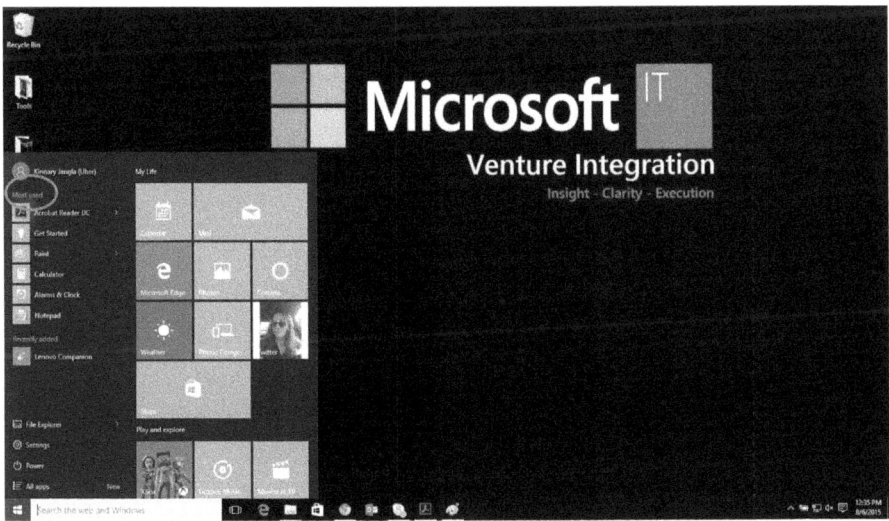

Figure 2-15. The most recently used apps are placed under the Most Used section

You can also unpin an item from the Most Used section if you don't like seeing it there or the long list of apps seems too cluttered. Selecting the **Don't show in this list** option (see Figure 2-16) takes an app away from the Most Used list.

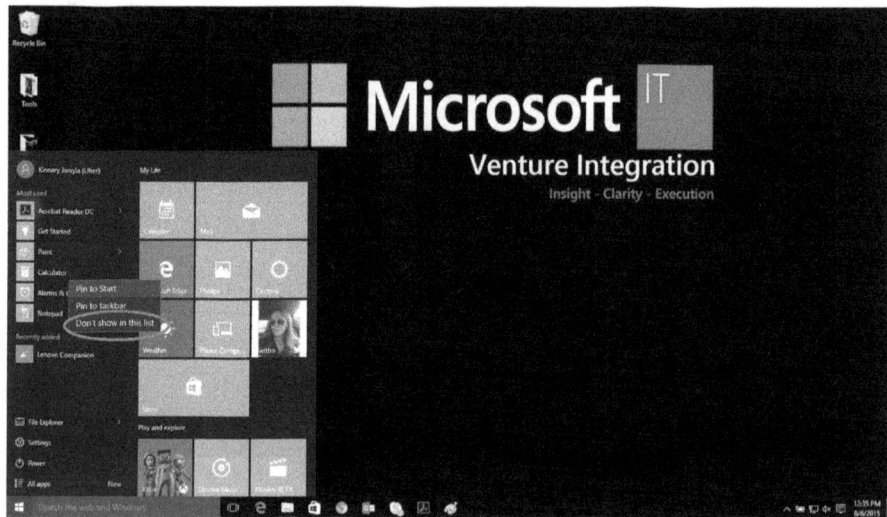

Figure 2-16. *Select "Don't show in this list" if you don't want the app to appear in the Most Used section*

Power Button

In Windows 8, the charms bar appeared on the right side of the screen and had Power Options built into it. Windows 10 does not have the charms bar. The power button appears in the Start menu in the bottom-left side, above the hamburger menu for apps (see Figure 2-17). It has the **Sleep**, **Shut down**, and **Restart** options.

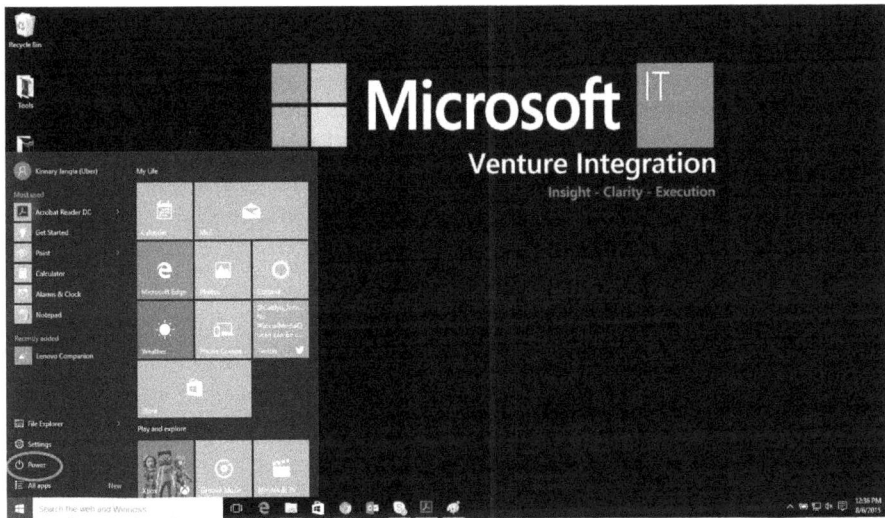

Figure 2-17. *The power button is on the bottom-left side of the Start menu*

Quick Options

Right-clicking the Windows icon (the Start menu icon) brings up a very useful context menu that gives you access to a Jump List to directly open items such as the Control Panel, Task Manager, File Explorer, and so forth, as seen in Figure 2-18.

Figure 2-18. *Right-click the Windows icon (Start menu icon) to see the Jump List*

41

Swipe Gestures

In Windows 10, Microsoft introduces several three-finger swipe gestures. Also, the single-finger swipe gestures from the left and right of the screen have different functions now. The following lists the different swipe gestures available in Windows 10.

- A three-finger downward swipe on the trackpad minimizes all of your active windows. A three-finger upward swipe on the trackpad brings them back up.

- A three-finger left and right swipe on the trackpad lets you switch between open apps.

- The Task View feature is a very interesting feature introduced in Windows 10 that allows you to look at the open apps on your desktop. This can also be done by selecting the Task View feature icon on the taskbar, as seen in Figure 2-19).

Figure 2-19. *The Task View feature on the taskbar*

Wrapping It Up

In this chapter, I focused on Windows 10 for tablets and desktops. Although the unifying experience of Windows 10 gives you a similar experience on all devices, this chapter focuses on features that you are more likely to use on a tablet or a PC. I explained the Continuum feature in Windows 10. I discussed the new revamped Start menu and all the different things that you can do with it. I also showed you the different swipe gestures available in Windows 10.

CHAPTER 3

Cortana and Edge

In this chapter, I show you how to use Microsoft's intelligent personal digital assistant, Cortana, and the new browser, Edge. Both come with a huge amount of built-in features to make your life easier and fun. Cortana is a very clever assistant that helps you find things on the Web and on the PC. It keeps track of your appointments and reminders, and even tells you jokes. Microsoft Edge is the brand-new browser by Microsoft. It comes with a bunch of handy and fun features. First, I show you some of Cortana's cool features and how to use them to increase your productivity. After that, I show you the unique features of the Edge browser. Finally, I wrap it up by showing you how Cortana and Edge perform so well together.

In this chapter, I focus on how and where to locate Cortana on your device, how to use her for different day-to-day commands, and how to customize her per your likes—all with the help of screenshots. After that I show you how the Edge browser is different from the age-old Internet Explorer, as well as all the unique features—again with the help of screenshots. Both Cortana and Edge work exactly the same way on all of your Windows 10 devices. So everything holds true for phones, tablets, and PCs.

Table 3-1 provides a summary of this chapter.

Table 3-1. *Chapter Summary*

Problem	Figures
Cortana	3-1 to 3-17
Microsoft Edge	3-18 to 3-29
Cortana and Edge together	3-30 to 3-31

© Kinnary Jangla 2015
K. Jangla, *Windows 10 Revealed*, DOI 10.1007/978-1-4842-0686-7_3

☰ **Note**   Microsoft Edge was called "Project Spartan" until the Windows 10 technical preview 2. So if you have the technical preview installed on your device, search for Project Spartan instead of Microsoft Edge. Remember, they are the same thing.

Cortana

Cortana is the clever new digital assistant on your Windows 10 device. You can speak to her, ask her different questions, and even train her to do some of your chores. The more you use Cortana, the more she will learn about you. She becomes trained to your needs and gets continuously better at helping you as an everyday assistant. Cortana can chat with you, answer your questions, get information for you, and even do things for you. Cortana's Notebook keeps track of what you like and what you want her to do. You can edit her Notebook to add and remove stuff. You can add your favorite eating places, set your reminders, and add the places you usually visit, your favorite stocks, music, travel destinations, and so forth. If Cortana doesn't know the answer to your question, she will Bing it for you and show you the results.

Finding Cortana

This section explains where and how you can find the Cortana app on your device.

1.   On your Windows 10 phone, search for Cortana in the apps list if you don't see it on your Start screen (see Figure 3-1).

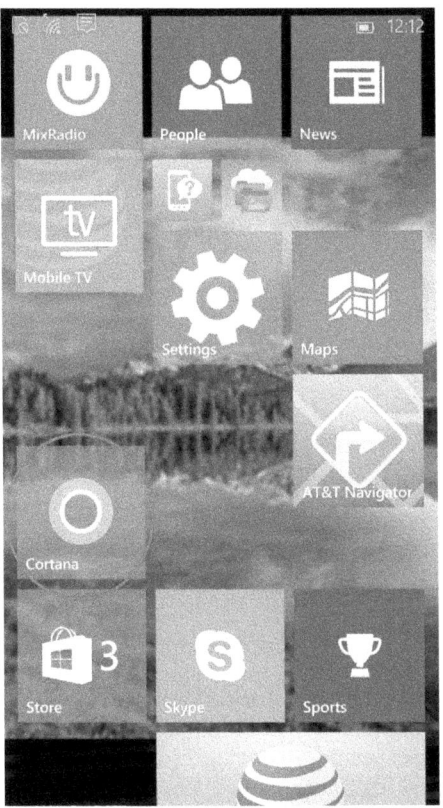

Figure 3-1. *Cortana on the Start screen of Windows Phone 10*

2. On your tablet or PC, you should see the **Ask me anything** text box on the left side of your taskbar (see Figure 3-2). That's Cortana.

Figure 3-2. *Cortana on a Windows 10 tablet*

Using Cortana

Cortana can be used for a varied set of commands. This speech assistant comes in really handy when you don't want to type in stuff or you want to search for things more quickly than usual. For instance, I find that Cortana is great while I'm driving. I can ask her to text a friend by simply telling her to do so, or I can ask her for directions without having to go to the Maps app and searching for it myself. I can ask her general-knowledge questions or to change my calendar appointments. I can even ask her to remind me of an event or change the details of my event. And finally, I can just casually chat with her and ask her to tell me a joke or two!

The following are examples of some of the commands that you can give Cortana:

- Give me directions to Yellowstone.

- How many calories are there in a cup of black beans?

- Change my appointment from 3 p.m. to 4 p.m.

- Message Bob to tell him I'm on my way.

- Tell me a joke.

You can activate Cortana by pressing the microphone button in the **Ask me anything** text box or by saying, "Hey, Cortana." She starts listening as soon as she hears that (see Figure 3-3).

Figure 3-3. *Cortana starts listening when you select the microphone icon or say "Hey, Cortana."*

Now let's see how Cortana behaves when she listens to some of these commands.

- Command: "Give me directions to Yellowstone." (see Figure 3-4).

Hi, Kin.

give me directions to yellowstone   →

Figure 3-4. *Ask Cortana for directions to Yellowstone*

Cortana locates Yellowstone on the default Bing Maps, as seen in Figure 3-5.

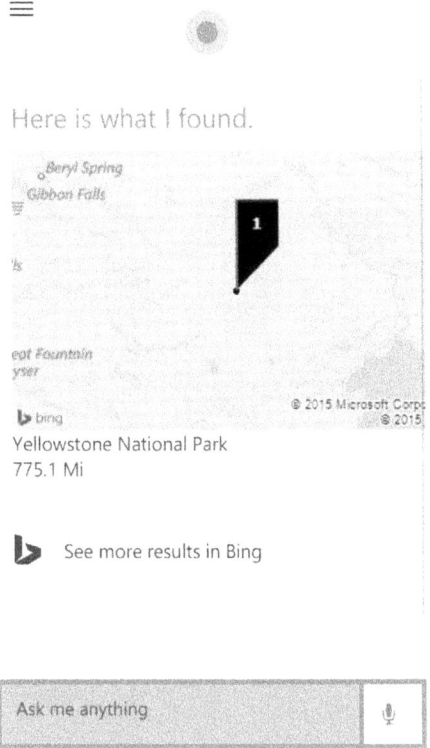

Figure 3-5. *Cortana shows Yellowstone on the default Bing Maps. You can click it to get directions*

- Command: "Text Bob I'm on my way."

   Cortana confirms by sending a text message to Bob, as seen in Figure 3-6. This feature really comes in handy when you want to send a message to someone while you're driving, for instance.

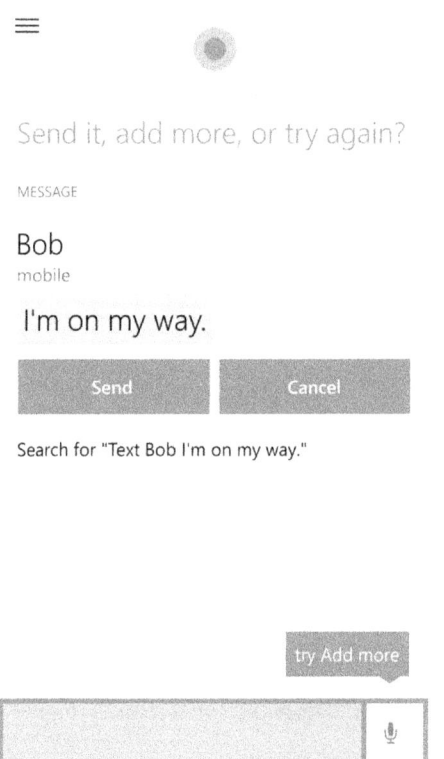

Figure 3-6. *Sending a text message to a contact*

- Command: "How does my weekend look?"

  Cortana looks at your Calendar and brings up all of your weekend appointments (see Figure 3-7).

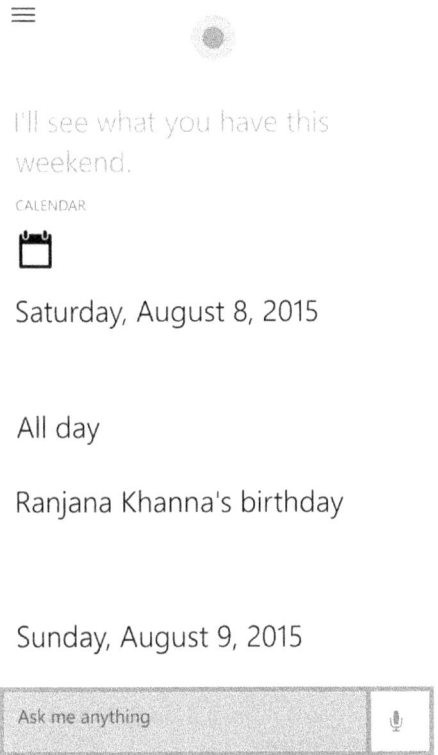

I'll see what you have this weekend.

CALENDAR

Saturday, August 8, 2015

All day

Ranjana Khanna's birthday

Sunday, August 9, 2015

Ask me anything

Figure 3-7. Cortana brings up your weekend appointments

- Command: "Add an appointment tomorrow from 3 p.m. to 4 p.m. to meet with Joe." (see Figure 3-8).

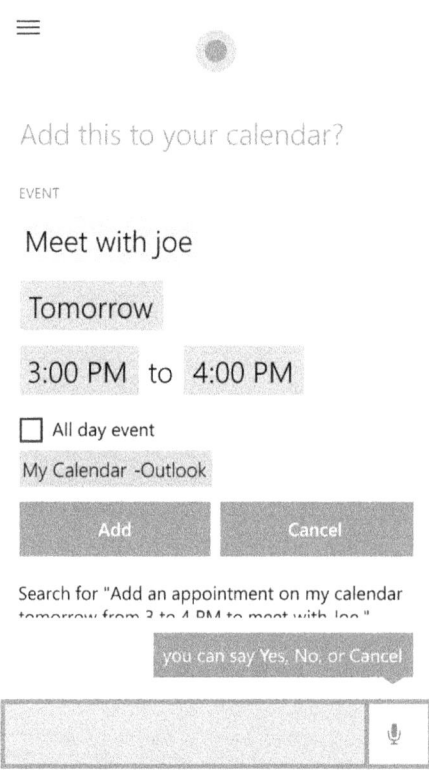

Figure 3-8. Cortana adds a new appointment to your calendar

- Command: "How many calories are there in a cup of black beans?" (see Figure 3-9).

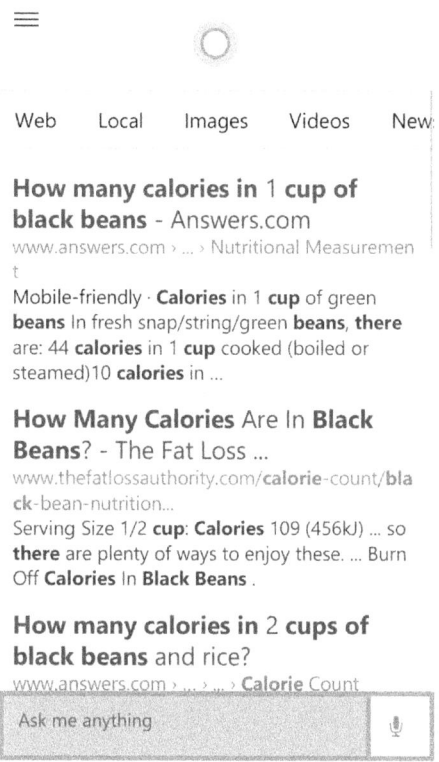

Figure 3-9. *Cortana searches using Bing and brings up results for calories in a cup of black beans*

- Command: "Tell me a joke." (see Figure 3-10).

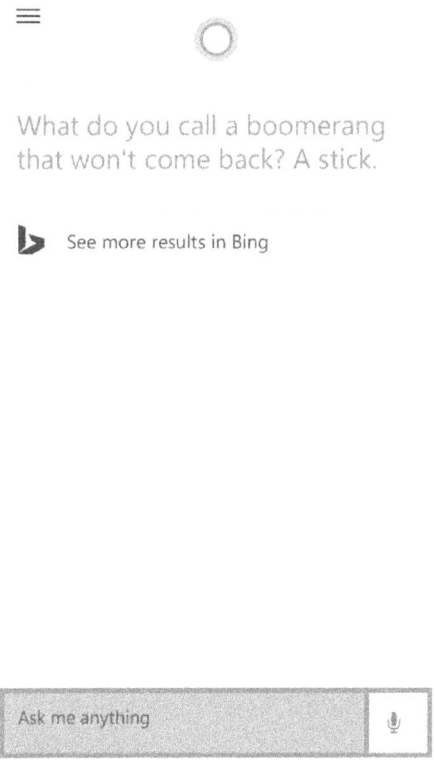

Figure 3-10. *Cortana tells you a joke!*

Customizing Cortana

In the "Using Cortana" section, I showed you how to use Cortana with its default settings. Here I show you how you can customize Cortana according to your likes. There are different settings to let you add your favorite things, so Cortana can learn more about you. Like I mentioned, Cortana uses a structured Notebook to keep track of your interests. The more information that you give Cortana, the better she can serve you. She is continuously learning from all the information you provide her. There are several things you can add to her Notebook, such as favorite restaurants, favorite music, reminders, travel itineraries, appointments, movies, stocks, and so forth. You can also set quiet hours so that she knows when you don't like to be disturbed. There are separate tabs on Cortana's main menu for places and music.

Adding a Category Interest in the Notebook

In this section, I show you how to add a category of interest in Cortana's Notebook.

1. In your Cortana app, select the icon in the top-right corner (see Figure 3-11).

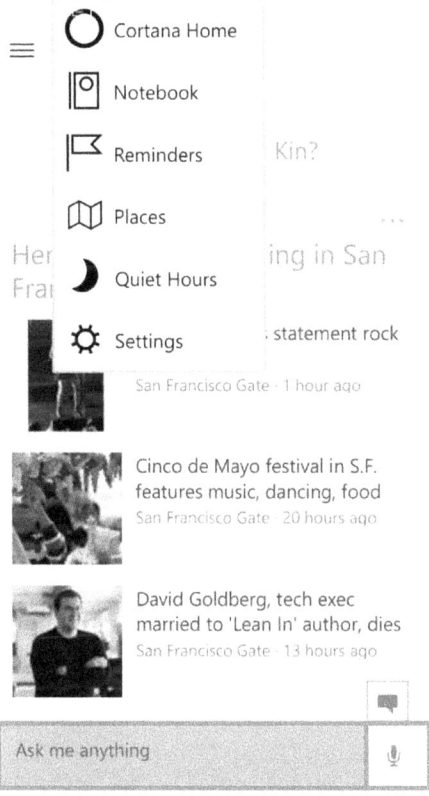

Figure 3-11. *Select the icon in the top-right corner to go to Cortana's Notebook*

2. From the context menu, select **Notebook**. You'll see everything in Cortana's Notebook; this is where she learns things. Selecting the **add** (+) icon lets you add a category (of your choice) to the Notebook, as seen in Figure 3-12.

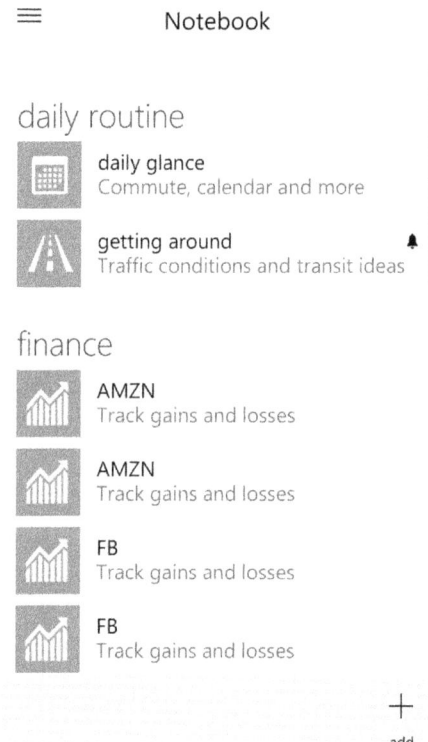

Figure 3-12. *Cortana's Notebook*

3. Select a category of your choice and add it to Cortana's Notebook (see Figure 3-13).

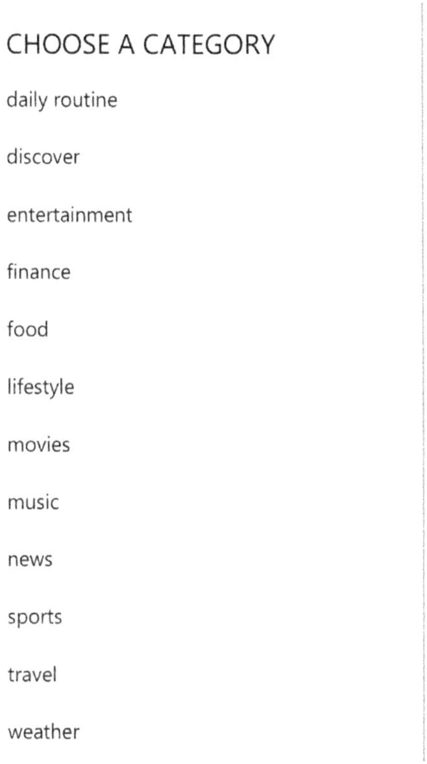

CHOOSE A CATEGORY

daily routine

discover

entertainment

finance

food

lifestyle

movies

music

news

sports

travel

weather

Figure 3-13. *Select a category of interest*

4.   Choose an interest from that category. (Here I chose food, as seen in Figure 3-14.)

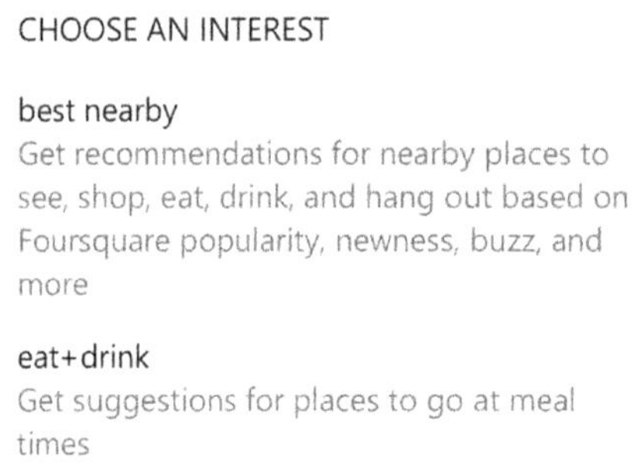

CHOOSE AN INTEREST

best nearby
Get recommendations for nearby places to
see, shop, eat, drink, and hang out based on
Foursquare popularity, newness, buzz, and
more

eat+drink
Get suggestions for places to go at meal
times

Figure 3-14. *Select an interest from the selected category*

Adding a Place

You can also add a place directly from the context menu in shown Figure 3-11.

1. Once you select **Places**, select the **add** (+) icon on the
    bottom-right corner, as seen in Figure 3-15.

+
add

Figure 3-15. *Select the add icon in the bottom-right corner in the Places window*

2. Selecting the **add** (+) icon lets you search for a place of interest and suggests places accordingly. In the screen that follows, you can give the place a nickname for easy future reference, as seen in Figure 3-16.

Figure 3-16. *Search for the place of interest*

3.   Once you've added a place, you will see it in your Favorites (see Figure 3-17). You can also edit or delete the place.

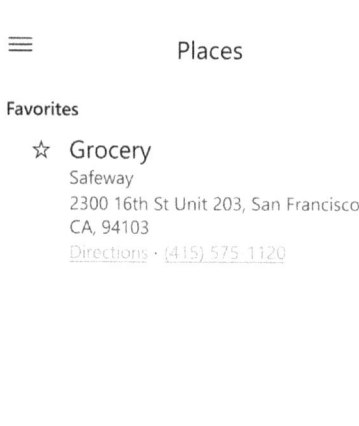

Figure 3-17. *The place is saved in your Favorites*

You can do similar things in Reminders and Music.

Microsoft Edge

Microsoft Edge is a brand-new browser with a fresh new engine that's completely different than the famous old Internet Explorer. Edge is bundled up with some really fresh, cool, and fun features that are excellent at increasing your productivity. Edge has all the basic browser functionality, along with many cooler features. Next I show you how to do all the cool things that Edge offers.

Searching Faster in Your Address Bar

With the new Edge browser, you can quickly search for things by using the little search icon built into the address bar. Just type keywords, and the results and suggestions show up in a snippet, as seen in Figure 3-18.

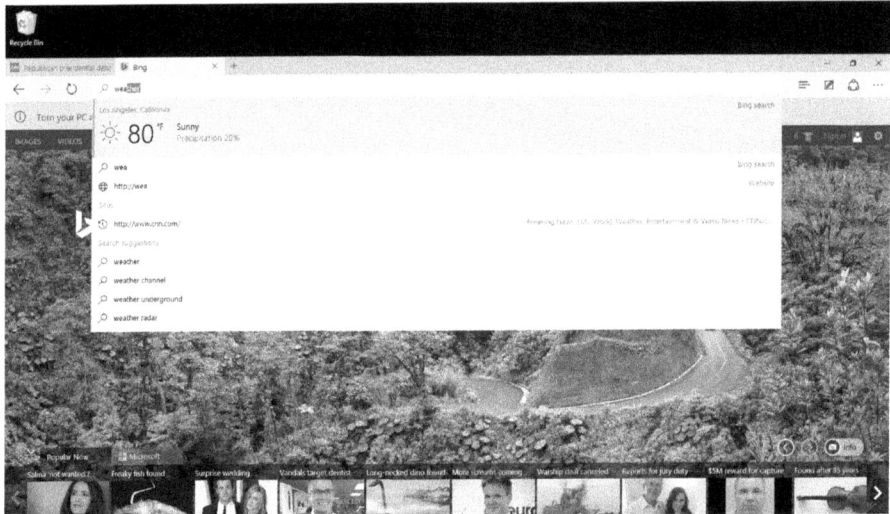

Figure 3-18. *Quickly search for weather in Edge's address bar*

Hub: The One-Stop Place for All of Your Favorites

Hub lets you store your favorite articles and also lets you take your Reading List wherever you travel. The Reading List lets you save your web pages offline so that you can read them later without Internet connectivity; it also synchronizes them across multiple devices. It makes accessing your browsing history super simple. It also shows you your downloaded items on one quick tab.

1. Select the Hamburger menu (see Figure 3-19) to go to the Hub.

Figure 3-19. *Click the Hamburger menu to go to your favorites*

2. To add a link to your Favorites, select the star icon on the address bar (see Figure 3-20). The menu that pops up gives you the option of adding it to your Favorites or to your Reading List (see Figure 3-21). Adding it to your Favorites saves the link in the Favorites tab in the Hub; adding it to the Reading List saves the link in the Reading List tab in the Hub.

Figure 3-20. *Select the star icon in the address bar. You can add the link to Favorites or to the Reading list*

63

Figure 3-21. *Selecting the star icon in the address bar lets you add a link to your Reading List*

You can view your Reading List by selecting the Reading List icon in the Hub (see Figure 3-22).

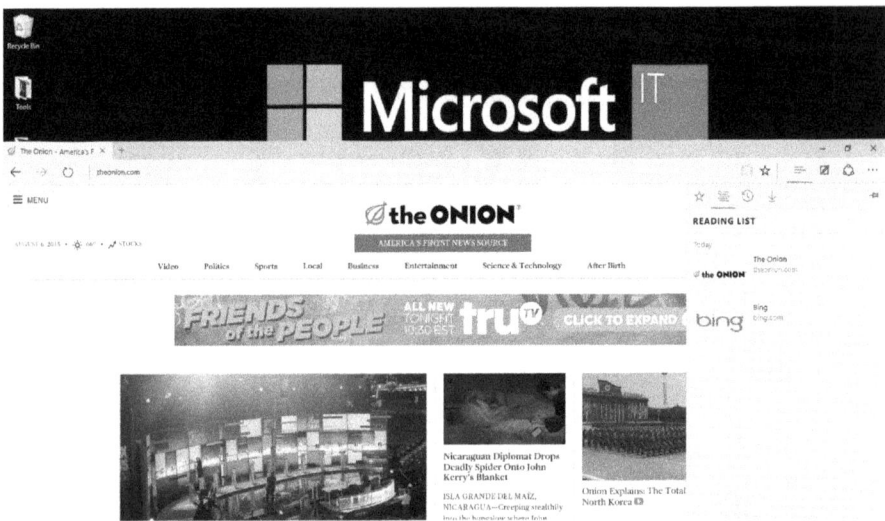

Figure 3-22. *View the Reading List in the Hub*

You can view your recent downloads by selecting the download icon in the Hub (see Figure 3-23).

Figure 3-23. *Select the download icon from the Hub to view your downloads*

Write on the Web

Microsoft Edge lets you make notes, highlight, draw, and comment on the Web. It then lets you share this with people. So you can share a secret note with someone, or a secret chef recipe with someone else. Next I show you how you can write on a web page and share it.

1. Select the **Make a Web Note** icon in the area to the right of the address bar (see Figure 3-24).

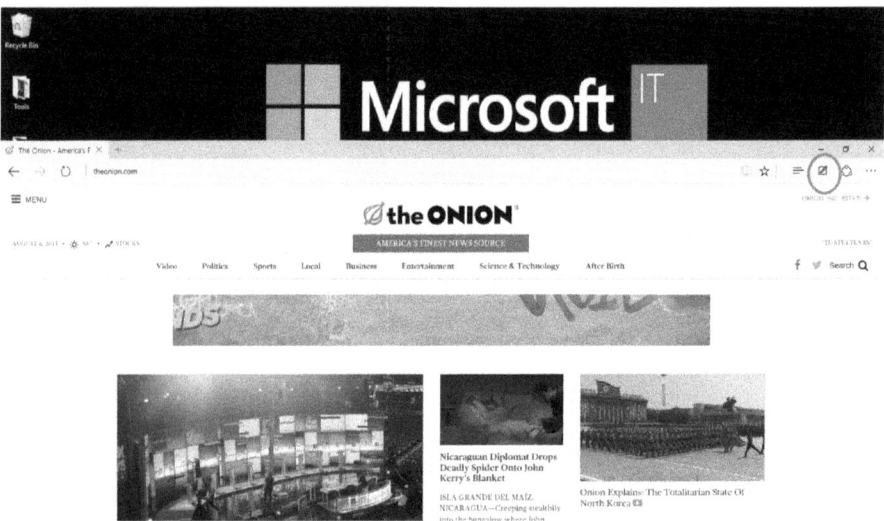

Figure 3-24. *Select the "Make a Web Note" icon to write on the Web*

2. You will see an edit bar appear in place of the address bar (see Figure 3-25).

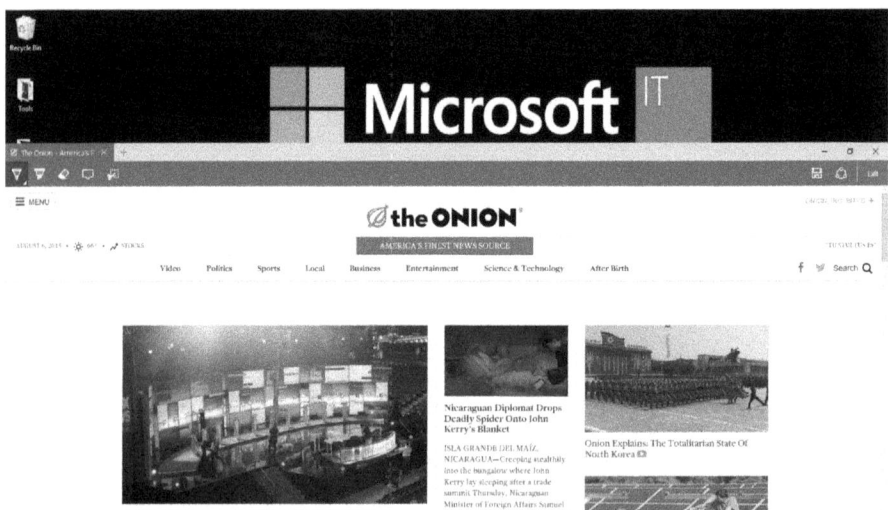

Figure 3-25. *The edit bar appears on top of the web page*

3. You can select the highlighter or the pen icon and choose a color to highlight or to start making notes (see Figure 3-26).

Figure 3-26. *Select the color of your choice to start making notes*

4. You can even make notes on a web page by selecting the text-box icon (see Figure 3-27).

Figure 3-27. *Make notes and highlight sections*

5. You can save the page by selecting the save icon. You share by going to the menu below **Exit** and selecting the **Share** option (see Figure 3-28).

Figure 3-28. *Share the web page by selecting the Share option from the menu*

Enabling the Reading View

The Edge browser lets you read free of distractions. To enable the Reading view, select the read icon in the address bar. Your article appears clean and noise-free (see Figure 3-29).

Figure 3-29. *The Reading view in the Edge browser*

░ **Note**   All the screenshots for the Microsoft Edge browser were taken from a tablet. It behaves exactly the same on the Windows Phone 10 and PCs.

Cortana and Edge Combo

The Cortana and Edge duo is extra the one of the most productive things that you can get out of the Windows 10 operating system. This dynamic duo works together so well that it saves you tons of time and effort. Cortana sits in the Edge address bar, or in a right-click of highlighted text. She helps you understand the meaning of a word while you're reading, or helps you make reservations, for example. Next I show you some scenarios where the Edge and Cortana combination works beautifully.

░ **Note**   To use this feature, you will have to enable this setting by going to Hamburger menu on Edge → Settings → Advanced Settings and then turn on "Have Cortana assist me in Microsoft Edge".

---

1. To enable a Cortana search while reading an article in the Edge browser, simply select the Cortana search button (see Figure 3-2) in the address bar, or right-click after selecting a word (see Figure 3-30). Cortana searches Bing for you and shows you the results on a vertical tab alongside.

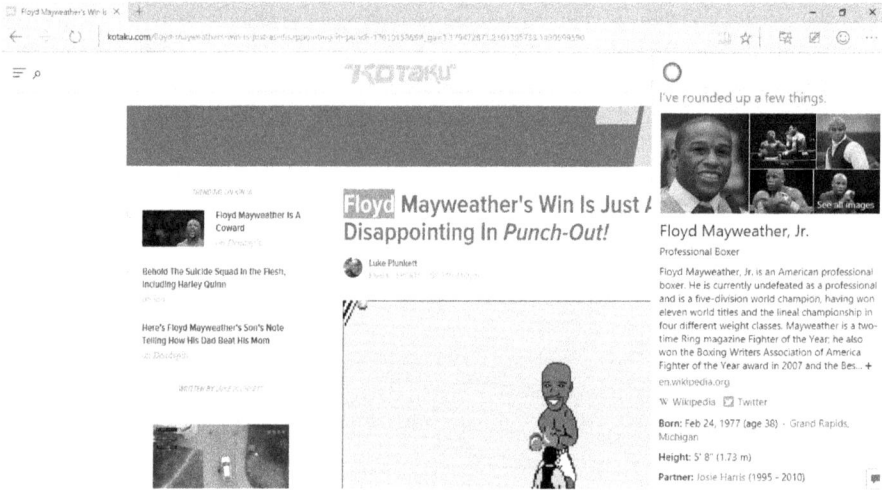

Figure 3-30. Cortana searches for the highlighted term on Bing and displays results alongside

2. Cortana can also help you make reservations when you come across an interesting restaurant; she can also show you the restaurant's hours and phone number, and provide directions to it (see Figure 3-31).

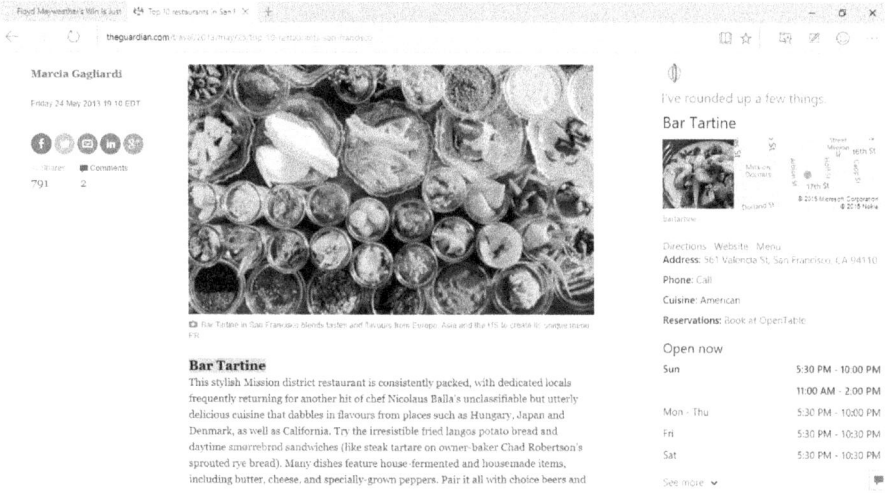

Figure 3-31. Cortana pulls up the hours, directions, phone number, and address, and lets you make reservation directly from the web page

Wrapping It Up

In this chapter, I showed you how to use Cortana on your Windows 10 device. I also showed you how to customize Cortana to meet your everyday needs. Later in the chapter I discussed Microsoft Edge and showed you all the features unique to this browser. I showed you how you can take your reading wherever you go by adding articles to the Reading List, how to read an article in the Reading view without distractions, and how to write on the Web and share your notes. Finally, I showed you how the dynamic duo of Cortana and Edge can do amazing things to make your life so much easier.

CHAPTER 4

Universal Apps

In this chapter, I show you how to use the different universal apps in Windows 10. But before I get into that, let me explain what a universal app means. A universal app is an app that works similarly across all Windows 10 devices, namely the phone, PC, and tablet. For developers, this means an app can be written once to run on a variety of devices. In this book, I do not go into the details of the development of universal apps. I stick to the user-facing features. As I have emphasized in previous chapters, Windows 10 is all about providing the user a unifying experience across devices; a universal app stands true to that. The convergence of all platforms running on one unified Windows core enables a single app to run on different devices. So the same app can run on your PC, your tablet, and on your Windows Phone. In all the previous versions of Windows, a single app would have different experiences on different Windows devices. Windows 10 gets rid of that, and gives the user a unifying experience.

In this chapter, I show you how some of these universal apps look and feel exactly the same on all of your devices, because they are the same app running everywhere. I show you what is new with the Mail, Calendar, Photos, Music, and People apps, as well as some of the Microsoft Office apps.

In this chapter, I am going to show you how to tell whether an app is a universal app or not, show you some of the universal apps that come built-in with the Windows 10 platform, and tell you what's new with them. I am going to cover the Mail app and Calendar app, and tell you about their new features. Later I show you the fun and cool Photos and Music apps. I then go into the People app to show you the new things that you can do with it. I also show you how to sync all your photos into one location. At the end, I focus on the Office apps, particularly Word and PowerPoint, which also work exactly the same way on all of your devices. I use Windows 10 tablet screenshots, but please bear in mind all the apps look and feel the same on all of your Windows 10 devices (per the Continuum feature).

Table 4-1 provides a summary of this chapter.

© Kinnary Jangla 2015
K. Jangla, *Windows 10 Revealed*, DOI 10.1007/978-1-4842-0686-7_4

Table 4-1. *Chapter Summary*

Problem	Figures
How to tell whether it is a universal app or not	4-1 to 4-2
Mail and Calendar apps	4-3 to 4-15
Photos app	4-16 to 4-19
Music and Videos apps	N/A
Microsoft Office apps	N/A

■ **Note**   I use Windows 10 tablet screenshots throughout this chapter. As the definition of universal apps holds, all of these apps look the same on all Windows 10 devices.

How to Tell Whether It Is a Universal App or Not

There is a neat little icon to identify universal apps; it looks like a computer and a phone overlapping each other. This icon represents the sharing experience, which is unifying across devices. When you search for an app in Windows Store, the app snippet shows you the icon to determine whether it is a universal app or not, as seen in Figure 4-1.

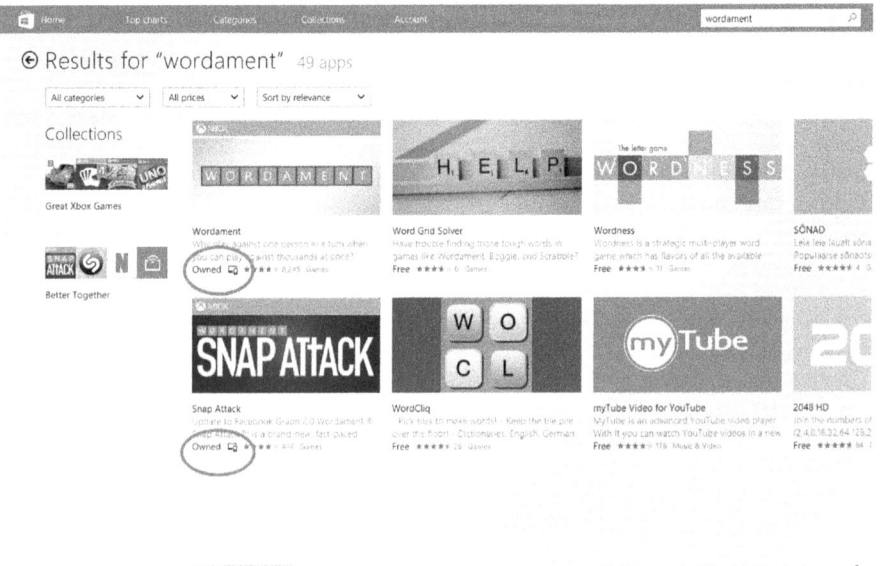

Figure 4-1. *Universal apps have the icon of a computer and a phone*

Furthermore, when you select the app, Figure 4-2 shows that you can see the icon on the following screen. The icon is clearly seen in Figure 4-3.

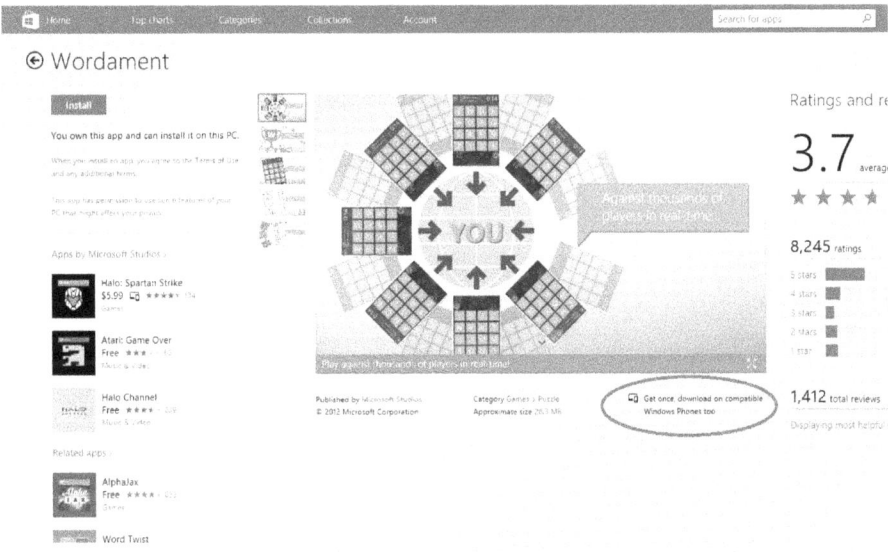

Figure 4-2. *The icon identifies a universal app*

Figure 4-3. *The universal app icon (a phone overlapping a computer)*

Mail and Calendar Apps

The new Mail app brings all of your e-mail accounts into one place, similar to what the desktop mail client has been doing. Of course, this is different than the current "link inboxes" function in Windows Phone 8.1. This new Mail app is universal and behaves in the same way across devices.

75

Upon opening the Mail app, you are welcomed with a clean-looking screen, like the one seen in Figure 4-4.

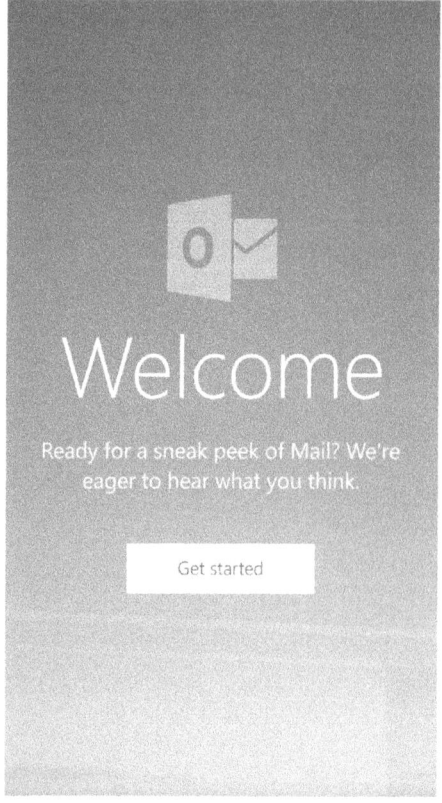

Figure 4-4. *The Welcome screen of the Mail app*

The **Get started** button takes you to the account screen that you already have on your phone, or the **Add account** screen, where you can add an account, as seen in Figure 4-5.

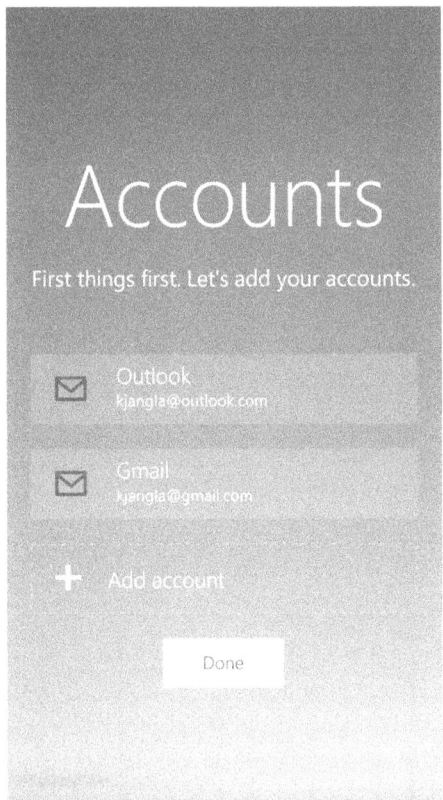

Figure 4-5. *The "Add account" screen on the Mail app*

Once you are inside the account, the screen looks really clean and the features are very intuitive. The compose mail button is in the top-right, alongside the refresh and the search buttons (see Figure 4-6).

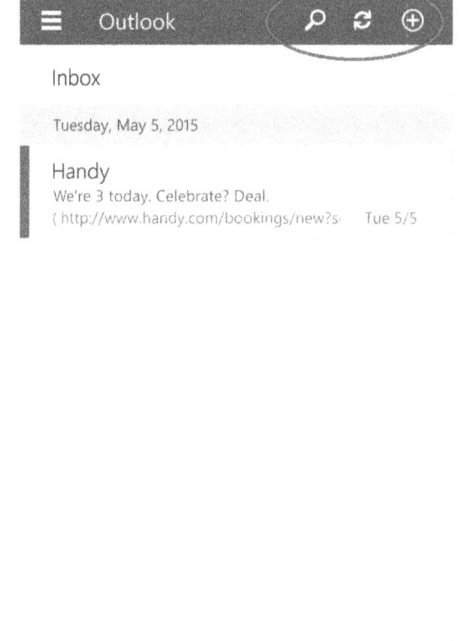

Figure 4-6. The compose mail, refresh, and search buttons are all on the top right

Going to the left side of the screen, and selecting the hamburger menu takes you to the Inbox, Drafts, and Sent Items (see Figure 4-7).

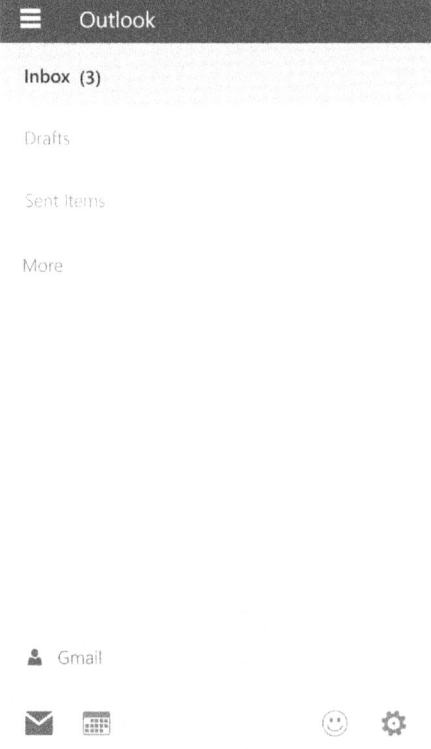

Figure 4-7. *Selecting the hamburger menu icon takes you the list of folders in your Inbox*

Deleting and flagging e-mails is super simple. A right swipe deletes an e-mail and a left swipe flags the e-mail. You don't need to go to a menu anymore to find these features (see Figures 4-8 and 4-9).

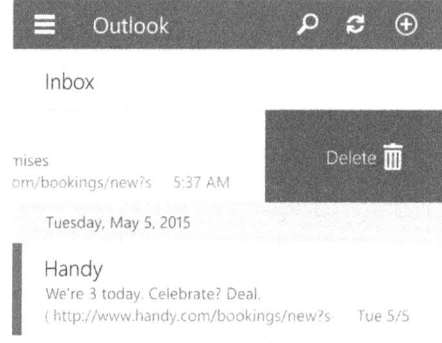

Figure 4-8. A right swipe deletes an e-mail

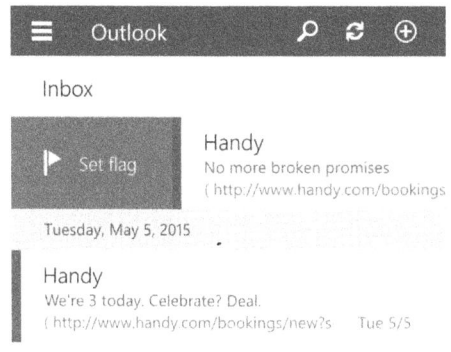

Figure 4-9. *A left swipe flags an e-mail*

To clear the flag, swipe left on the flagged e-mail (see Figure 4-10).

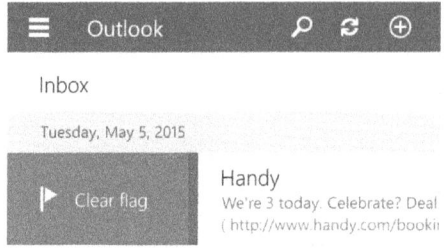

Figure 4-10. *Clear the flag on a previously flagged e-mail*

To get to the Calendar app, you can either access it from your Mail app or from the app list. From your Mail app, select the hamburger menu icon on the left side of the screen. You will see the Calendar icon on the bottom. Figures 4-11 and 4-12 show how to locate the Calendar app from the Mail app.

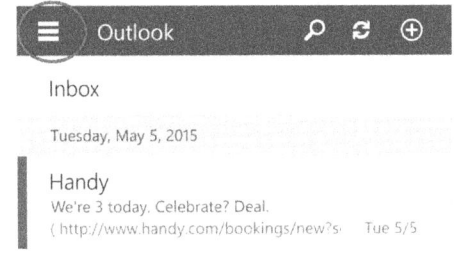

Figure 4-11. Select the icon on the top left of the screen

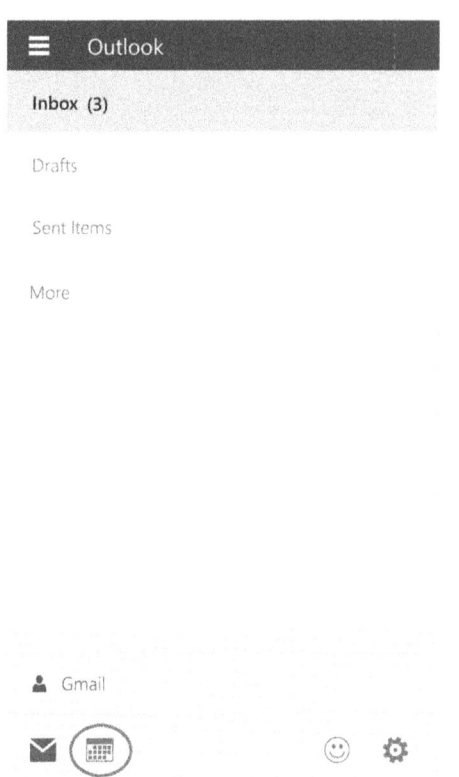

Figure 4-12. *The Calendar icon at the bottom of the screen*

Another way to go to the Calendar app is to find it in your app list. The app is called Outlook Calendar (see Figure 4-13).

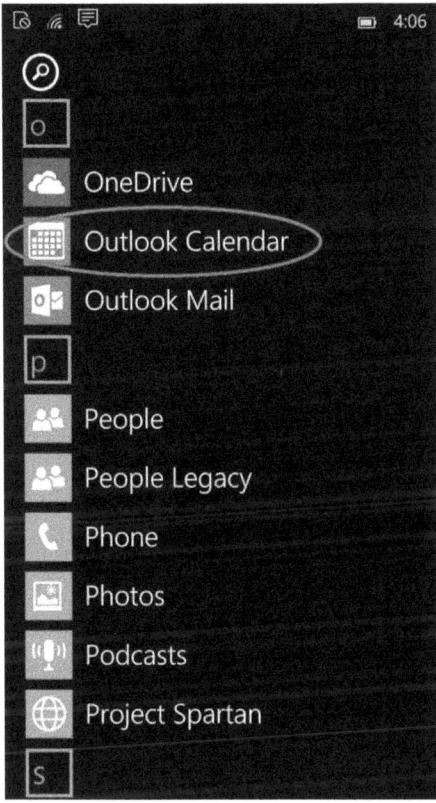

Figure 4-13. *Open the Calendar app from the app list*

As with the Mail app, the Calendar app welcomes you with a Welcome screen. After hitting the **Get started** button, if you've already added your account, you are presented with the new design of the Calendar (see Figure 4-14). Here you will find the current week laid out in Calendar view, with your appointments for the day underneath.

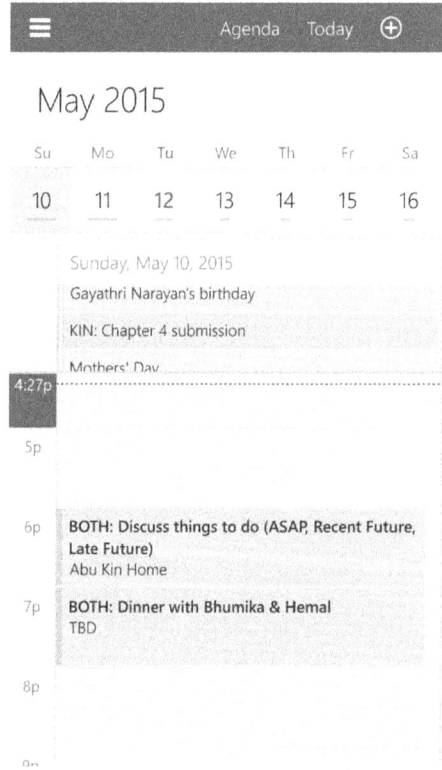

Figure 4-14. *The Day view design of the Calendar app. The Agenda, Today and Create an Event tabs are on the top of the screen*

At the top you have three buttons that change back and forth from the Agenda view and Day view. One takes you to today's date, and the other to create a new event.

Again, in the top-left corner, you have the hamburger menu. There you get a panel that allows you to turn off and on the various calendars you have for each account. You also have the feedback and settings buttons at the bottom of the Mail app (see Figure 4-15).

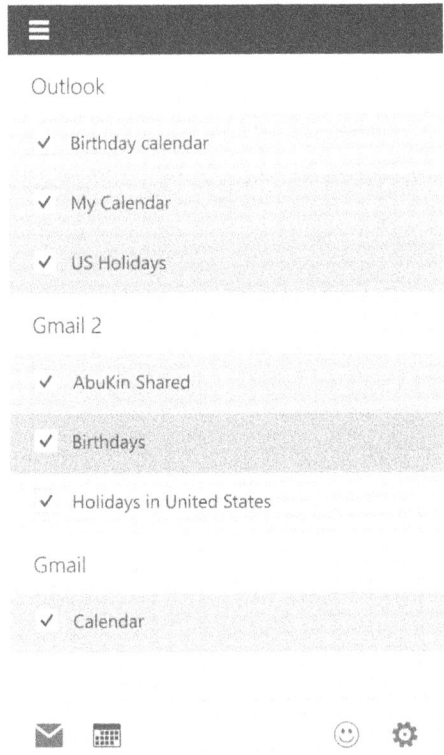

Figure 4-15. *The hamburger menu has a panel that allows you to choose which calendars you want on or off*

Finally, the dates slider shows you extra the all the days of the month (see Figure 4-16).

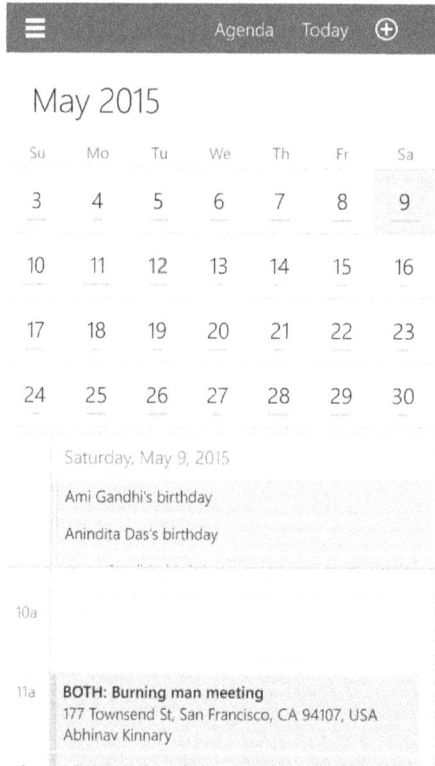

Figure 4-16. *A gentle top or bottom swipe on the dates slider shows you all the days of the month*

Photos App

The Organization feature in the Photos app is one of my favorite features. The Photos app aggregates all of your photos on your device and those on OneDrive, and offers a Collection view that sorts out any photos that may have been taken during burst mode, in this era of selfies. Also, you can choose to let the app create autogenerated photo albums or you can create your own. The visual effect is extremely attractive. The Collection view arranges the photos according to the dates on which they were taken. Figure 4-17 shows this feature.

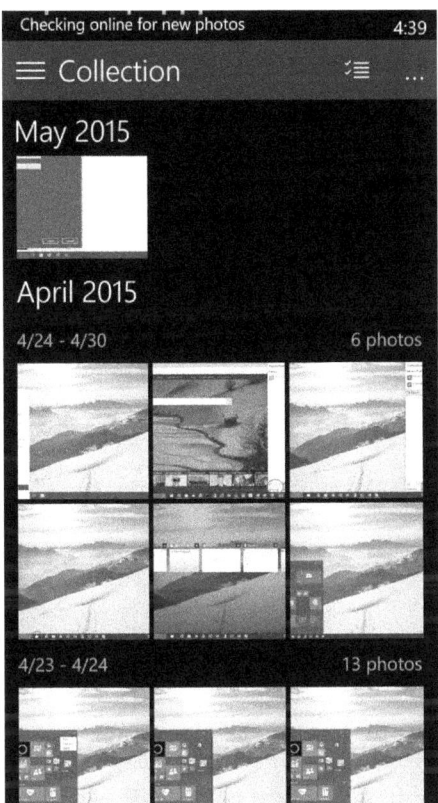

Figure 4-17. *The Collection view separates photos according to the dates that they were taken*

The Albums view automatically creates albums for you. Figure 4-18 shows the Albums view.

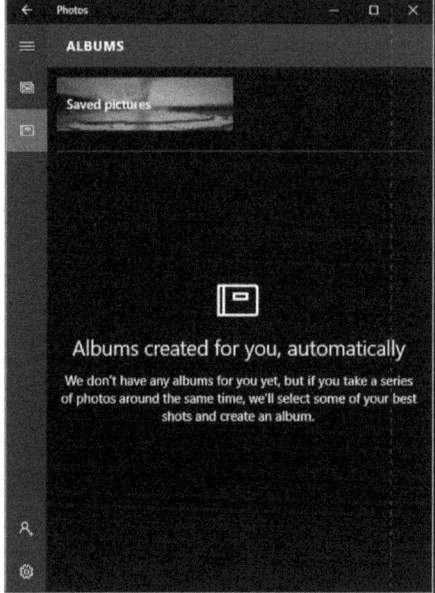

Figure 4-18. *This is a placeholder screenshot*

The hamburger menu in the top-left corner of the Photos app provides a panel where you can choose which view you want to see your photos in (see Figure 4-19).

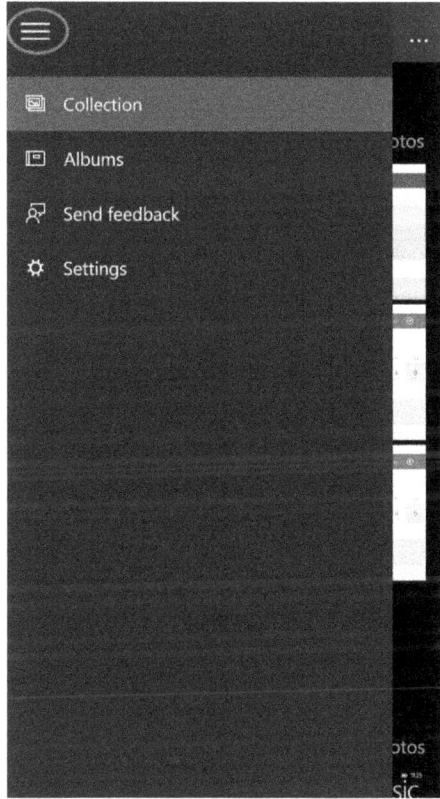

Figure 4-19. *The hamburger menu gives you the Collection and Album view options along with Feedback and Settings*

There is an Enhance button on the bottom of each photo; it enhances the colors and the overall quality of the picture, allowing you to remove red eye and brighten dark photos with just one button. Figure 4-20 shows the enhance button. You can also crop a photo pretty easily. Note the Crop button at the bottom of Figure 4-20.

Figure 4-20. *The Crop, Enhance, and Rotate buttons beneath the photo*

One of my favorite things about this app is that the presentation is similar on both the Desktop mode and the Mobile mode, indicating Microsoft's attempt to truly offer a universal photo app experience.

Music and Videos Apps

The new universal Music app has cooler features, but no longer has the Xbox naming convention. Although the Music app is very similar to the previous version, it has some modifications that makes its usage more efficient. You can now drag and drop songs into your Music app from across devices, and play songs from your OneDrive. You can also make playlists by dragging and dropping songs from different devices. There is better support to browse and buy music from the Windows Store. You can also shuffle, filter, and sort through songs from different artists. Overall, the new Music app has a much better, cleaner, and more elegant design (with a dark color scheme), as well as easier navigation and better accessibility.

The Videos app lets you browse, play, filter, and sort video files, as well as add your own folder of videos to the collection. You can do the same for purchased movies and TV shows, and play and pause them across devices.

Microsoft Office Apps

The Word, Excel, and PowerPoint apps in Windows 10 have significantly improved—both in design and in functionality. The Office for Windows 10 universal apps support Microsoft's traditional ribbon menu design. The Reflow mode enhances the viewing of documents on smartphones and small tablets.

Animations in PowerPoint are hardware enabled. The new Office for Windows 10 apps also support wireless printing.

Wrapping It Up

In this chapter I defined and detailed the concept of universal apps and showed you what some of the built-in universal apps—such as Mail, Calendar, Photos, Music, and Videos—and the Office apps look like, and how to use them. I showed you the new design of these apps, and how they behave similarly across devices. I showed you the different features of the Mail and Calendar apps. I also showed you how your photos can be arranged in different ways and more efficiently. I explained how the Music and Videos apps are more powerful now, and extra the how the new Office apps work so well across all devices.

Index

GPSR Compliance
The European Union's (EU) General Product Safety Regulation (GPSR) is a set
of rules that requires consumer products to be safe and our obligations to
ensure this.

If you have any concerns about our products, you can contact us on

ProductSafety@springernature.com

In case Publisher is established outside the EU, the EU authorized
representative is:

Springer Nature Customer Service Center GmbH
Europaplatz 3
69115 Heidelberg, Germany